Pastoral Care and Liberation Praxis

Pastoral Care and Liberation Praxis

Studies in Personal and Social Transformation

edited by
Perry LeFevre
and
W. Widick Schroeder

Exploration Press

Chicago, Illinois

Printed in the United States of America

Exploration Press
Chicago Theological Seminary
5757 University Avenue
Chicago, Illinois 60637

ISBN: Cloth: 0-913552-31-3
Paper: 0-913552-32-1

Library of Congress Catalog Card Number: 85-80511

Preface

The papers in this volume deal with issues in personal and social transformation. They were written by doctor of ministry students at the Chicago Theological Seminary during the past decade.

These papers complement those published in a 1984 Exploration Press volume, *Spiritual Nurture and Congregational Development*. These two volumes are offered as a contribution to the literature on the theory and practice of ministry in the hope that they will contribute to the quest for excellence in ministry.

In the preface to earlier volume, the editors briefly considered the status of the literature on ministerial practice and outlined the theory informing the development of the doctor of ministry professional paper at the Chicago Theological Seminary. For the benefit of readers who have not seen that volume, those observations are reproduced here with minor revisions to introduce these papers.

Compared to the other professions, literature dealing with ministerial practice is sparse. Except in the areas of pastoral care and Christian education, much of the existing literature is more anecdotal and theoretically less rigorous than comparable material in the law, medicine, or social work.

A number of factors contribute to this situation. The variety of religious traditions in the United States and the wide range of educational expectations for clergy make a focus on common issues difficult. Local clergy associations rarely foster the sustained study of professional problems and rarely encourage their members to develop critical papers dealing with issues in professional ministry. Denominational bodies are somewhat more successful in stimulating such work, but their overall contribution to the development of a literature dealing with the practice of ministry is not great. Interdenominational work is very minimal, for co-operative structures to sustain such work are fragile.

In many theological schools, the area of practical theology is understaffed. The people in this field are overworked and are pressed to provide a minimum of field experience and theological reflection for their students. In many instances, substantial intellectual and professional distance exists between faculty persons in the fields of theology, Bible, and church history and faculty persons in the fields of homiletics, pastoral care, religious education, and parish studies.

The various faculty often have quite diverse scholarly interests, and they rarely give their co-ordinated attention to issues in the practice of ministry. The primary professional reference groups of the faculty in the various fields of a theological school are different, and this situation makes collaborative work on issues in the practice of ministry difficult. For many years the academic doctoral research model has dominated advanced work in theological institutions.

As just noted, pastoral care and religious education are the two areas in which the most work has been published. Professional societies in these areas have existed for over fifty years, and substantial bodies of professional literature have been developed in both areas. Although theoretical issues dealing with the relation of theology and the human sciences abound in these areas, the fields are relatively clearly delineated.

In the past decade or so, three developments have occurred which may well increase the development of critical reflections on the practice of ministry. First, several institutes dealing with a broad range of parish issues have been established and are promoting a wide range of parish focused studies. Second, the field of parish studies has evolved into a major area of interest, and many persons are expressing interest in it. Third, the emergence of numerous doctor of ministry programs in theological schools in the United States and Canada is heightening clergy interest in reflection on issues in the practice of ministry. Motivated both by the desire for enhanced competence in the practice of ministry and by the desire for a doctoral degree, clergy persons have been attracted to these programs in increasing numbers in the past ten years.

The Chicago Theological Seminary was among the first theological schools in the United States to develop a professional doctoral degree program. Since 1967 the seminary has offered a professional doctoral degree. Its program has attracted Protestant, Catholic and Jewish students from diverse cultural and national backgrounds. The Seminary has maintained an openness towards a wide variety of professional interests in ministry. Even though the papers reflect the particular backgrounds of their authors, they offer creative suggestions to others engaged in the varied ministries of our religious bodies.

In addition to the professional paper each doctoral student has written a position paper formulating his or her primal conviction about some facet of ministerial practice. These metatheoretical papers inform the professional papers, but the professional papers address ministerial practice more explicitly than do the position papers.

The elective and common elements in the program have varied over the years, but the focal point for each doctoral student has been the professional paper that addresses some problem in the practice of ministry. The topic may be embodied in either one's own or someone else's practice of ministry. The practice being examined may be either that of a contemporary or an historical figure or institution.

The professional doctoral degree at the Chicago Theological Seminary is designed to have an integrity of its own. It is distinct from the academic doctorate and is not an appendage to a master of divinity degree.

The professional paper illustrates this intent. Although it usually includes a research component, the paper is not a dissertation and is not a research document. It strives to enhance the practice of ministry, and it *must* address the implications of its findings for the practice of ministry. Ideally, the implications ought to be embodied in that practice and critically assessed.

The author defines the paper's primary audience, but that audience is commonly not a specialized research audience. In fact, most frequently the primary audience is one's colleagues engaged in the practice of ministry. Each author seeks to reflect critically on some facet of ministry and to communicate those reflections to one's professional colleagues.

After some experimentation, the seminary faculty limited the professional paper to twenty-five, double-spaced, typewritten pages. The limitation was imposed for two reasons. First, a professional journal rarely will consider a paper beyond that length. Second, the page limitation forces the author to focus sharply on the problem and to determine critically the salient factors to be included in the paper.

The persons writing these papers are not and do not intend to become research specialists in one of the human sciences, but they do want to use fitting human science theory and research methods to illumine the ministerial problems they are addressing. In all instances, the authors had to consider carefully the scale and the scope of their papers, for they constituted about a fifth of their work in the doctor of ministry program.

Readers of these papers should be mindful of the gifts and interests of the authors. The papers are designed primarily to stimulate the critical thinking and to enhance the professional competence of clergy persons in professional ministry. They are not merely studies *about* the practice of ministry in our time; they are studies *for* the practice of ministry in our time.

The doctor of ministry program strives to develop graduates who will continue to engage in critical self-reflection about the practice of ministry and to share their reflections with colleagues. While informal sharing in face-to-face groups has undoubtedly taken place, so far only a few graduates have published additional professional papers beyond the one required for the professional doctorate. This reality has been a disappointment, and we hope that more papers will be forthcoming in future years. The long term quality of the profession will be enhanced by clergy persons continuing to engage in critical assessments of the practice of ministry in our time. These assessments can be fostered by theological schools and denominational bodies and professional societies, but they must be actualized by clergy directly engaged in the practice of ministry with lay people.

The editors have selected approximately ten percent of the papers written by doctor of ministry candidates during the past decade for inclusion in this volume or in the preceding volume, *Spiritual Nurture and Congregational Development*. It was a difficult task to select these papers, for space limitations precluded the selection of more than a sampling of the papers. The editors sought papers of general interest and substantial scope that met the following criteria:

1) The problem addressed is a significant problem in the practice of ministry.
2) The theory guiding the interpretation and analysis of the problem is clear and coherent.
3) The problem is clarified by a relevant and fittingly inclusive research component.
4) The paper incorporates critical reflections on the implications of the examination of this problem for the enhancement of the practice of ministry.

The papers included in this volume center around topics in personal and social transformation. The first three papers address topics in personal transformation.

Gary S. Gerson uses family systems theory and notions derived from Martin Buber to interpret funeral ritual processes and advances a model to implement the theory. Because it has primarily a theoretical focus, it is unusual for a professional paper. It was accepted because the paper is to serve as the first section of a book which will develop the implications for practice in some detail.

Robert Hurst questions the adequacy of the "grief process model" for divorce adjustment counseling and reports on his spiritual direction approach to divorce counseling. Ann Bartram discusses four guidelines that have informed her responses to pastor-client sexual attraction and indicates her own therapeutic approach to sexual attraction in a counselling context through the use of a verbatim between her and one of her clients.

The other four papers deal with issues in social transformation and the quest for social justice. Because power—both linear and reciprocal—is more salient in intergroup relations than in interpersonal relations, the issues addressed are relatively more dynamic and more ambiguous than are the issues addressed in the first three papers. The authors of these papers are seeking very substantial transformation of existing social structures and/or public policies and are envisaging the concomitant personal transformation of persons enmeshed in these social structures.

Three of the papers in this section were informed by the transformative educational theories of Paulo Freire. Roy H. May, Jr. evaluates a program of community development in northeastern Brazil. Renny Golden describes and assesses an educational program carried out on the west side of Chicago. The program granted an accredited high school diploma to adults who had dropped out of school but was not as alienating as the Graduate Equivalency Diploma Program. Felix Sugirtharaj examines a program designed to liberate untouchables in South India villages.

In the fourth paper Steven F. Durham considers an effort sponsored by the Presbyterian Church to address the problem of political intimidation and assassination in Central America.

The papers included in this volume have not been revised stylistically. Consequently, there is some stylistic variation from paper to paper.

Taken together, *Spiritual Nurture and Congregational Development* and *Pastoral Care and Liberation Praxis* reflect many of the diverse issues of religious practice addressed by persons in the professional doctoral program since its inception at the Chicago Theological Seminary.

We hope that readers will be stimulated by these reflections on the practice of ministry and will find some material that will facilitate excellence in their own ministries. We also hope that readers will be stimulated to promote individual and peer critical reflection on issues of general interest in their own ministries.

Perry LeFevre
W. Widick Schroeder

Table of Contents

Pastoral Care and Liberation Praxis

Part One

Personal Transformation

CHAPTER I

Grief and Mourning

BY GARY S. GERSON

Wherefore all these last offices and ceremonies that concern the dead, the careful funeral arrangements, and the equipment of the tomb, and the pomp of obsequies, are rather the solace of the living than the comfort of the dead.

Augustine

Birth is a beginning and death a destination. And life is a journey. It is a process of changes, some small, some great: from moment to moment or place to place, from youth to age, from life to death.

Each change may also become a passage, an opportunity for transition and transformation, and because of this, a gift and an offering. This is no less true of mourning for a loved one, the most intense passage of all.

When one that we love has died, we grieve. We refuse to let go. We deny. We drive away those who would challenge our denial, or we retreat from them to avoid truth and to embrace unreality. Grief is an attempt to hold everything static and in one place.

But just as life is a process, so is grief. It is a process of stages which blend into and replace one another. From denial to distancing, from guilt to anxiety, from pining to depression, and then perhaps to acceptance. It is a process of pain which may be redeemed for the sake of growth. And though we may turn away from it, it will return to us over and over again until it is complete and has fulfilled its promise. Time is not enough. Grief must be worked at and worked out. That is why we do well to mourn -to allow our grief expression in ritual and behavioral ways. Mourning is a time of gestation out of which we may be reborn.

There is wisdom in the funeral and mourning ritual of traditional societies. Their's is a process that "works." Prescribed periods for mourning sanction when to begin and when to end grief. Sufficient time is given for mourning, often in a sequence of graduated time periods. Each period, in turn, is likely to have prescribed ritual practices appropriate to the characteristic duration and form of each stage of grieving. These require the active participation of all bereaved family members together with the whole community. One learns how to mourn and why, even as a child, and especially in one's family.

The Challenge To The Contemporary Funeral

Would that our funeral and mourning practices were as compelling as those of preliterate and traditional societies. Would that our vestigial death ceremonies were capable of promoting healing relation and the expression of grief in families where one has died. Unfortunately, they aren't.

In their study of the first year of bereavement, Glick, Weiss and Parkes found that if there is any benefit to leave-taking ceremonies, it is in the setting they provide. At their best, they may provide an opportunity for mourners to join with others in reflecting on the life of the one who has died, to offer one another support, and to reaffirm their continued ties. Beyond this, while mourners reported that the ceremonies were worthy of respect, they were essentially irrelevant to personal behavior. Those religious elements that were, in themselves, helpful were those that affirmed the continuation of the deceased in some fashion: either in the immortality of the soul or in that worthy deeds would live on.

Aside from officiating at the funeral and burial services, clergy contact was generally limited to a prefuneral exchange of information concerning the funeral and of data regarding the one who had died. Evidently few clergy attempted to give solace or counsel in a personal way. Of those mourners who spoke with clergy, the majority reported the meeting was neither helpful nor unhelpful.[1]

Rosenblatt, Walsh and Jackson concur with these findings in their cross-cultural study of grief and mourning. They also add that

> because many kin functions are carried out by other institutions in the United States, and because there is usually only an initial death ceremony [and hence no formal closure to mourning], the importance of death ceremonies in carrying out most functions is probably much less in the United States than elsewhere[2].

Death and mourning ceremonies in America are all too often vestigial and devoid of meaning. They are abbreviated, privatized, and often carefully hidden from children. They impart neither empathic understanding nor transformative knowledge. They do not provide for the resolution of grief or for the reorganization of self and family. They are form without substance. What little value they do have consists in the setting they provide for meeting and grieving, and in affirming the continuation of the deceased in some fashion.

Robert Moore writes that "a rather formidable argument could be advanced that the history of secularization in the Western culture can be read as a history of the decline and devaluing of ritual process."[3] In the modern world the rational and autonomous are valued at the expense of ritual performance and the interpersonal dimension of human life.

As rationalists, modern men and women tend to be a bureaucratic and technocratic. They are committed to the maintenance of a complex socio-economic, scientific and technological order. Hence they deny death, for death represents the unknown, the chaotic, the failure of scientific technology and the displacing of the rational by the non-rational. Death is pathological.

As a bureaucrat and technocrat, modern man or woman is urban and mobile. The extended family is an abstraction and a reality on only rare, short-lived occasions. So, too, community, which more and more refers to a spatial entity rather than to a social quality. Nuclear families are isolated, stressed and without sufficient external supports. And when there is a death within one, its members are frequently left to cope with their grief on their own if at all. When others do come to pay condolence calls, the transaction is often a "rip-off" to divert the mourners from their grief so no one has to acknowledge that one who was once present is no longer.

From time to time, a member of the clergy who has had enough of text-centered, pro forma funerals is moved to reflect on what really ought to go into a funeral service. In 1966, for example, both Edgar Jackson and Paul Irion published thoughtful discussions of the role of the funeral in the mourning process. Four years later, Jack Bloom wrote about how a eulogy can facilitate the grieving process by: affirming the reality of the death, addressing feelings of anger and guilt and confronting the loss of meaning in the patterns of the bereaved person's life. More recently, Dave McMahill has seen the potential for a funeral service to be a ministry celebrating the meanings in the life of the deceased and which thereby responds to the survivors' sense of meaninglessness. Unfortunately, few others have had such vision.[4]

In phone conversations, October of 1983, I questioned Rabbis Earl Grollman and Jack Reimer about this situation. Both men are acknowledged experts in the field of death, grief and mourning. Both men also confirmed my impression that little else has been written, and that what is being done by pulpit clergy to transvalue the funeral remains little known. It is in response to these conditions that this paper is being written.

The purpose of this paper is two-fold: it offers both a new theory of the funeral and a model of how that theory may be implemented. The theory is predicated on three assumptions: First, that grief is experienced and expressed by bereaved family systems as well as by bereaved individuals. Second, that the ritual process characteristic of funerals in traditional and preliterate society serves to promote empathy and consequently grief work by the family and a sense of transformation and growth. Third, that the one who has died may be evoked as a presence in memory. As this presence is made real in family dialogue and is confirmed in the eulogy, it acts as a conjoining and mediating agency. This agency confers power, meaning and grace for the work of grieving, reconciling and accommodating to mutual needs.

The implementing of this theory occurs during the two points in the funeral process when clergy and bereaved families are together, and at that one point when the community is present: during the prefuneral meeting and at the funeral service. There are three tasks in the prefuneral meeting: 1) to promote the emergence of communitas and empathic interaction among family members. This facilitates the expressing of grief. 2) to solicit family sharing of memories of the deceased as a Thou whereby the deceased may be evoked as a presence in memory. 3) to determine family structure, developmental stage and function in light of the death, and the family's self-understanding and its beliefs concerning what the deceased would want for them. All of this may suggest the tasks awaiting the family.

The eulogy is fashioned and offered at the funeral with four intentions: 1) to be an offering consecrating the memory of the one who has died as a Thou. The eulogy is sacred knowledge confirming the deceased as a presence that may be encountered in remembering and through one's actions. 2) to nurture family empathy 3) to articulate the tasks confronting the family in light of the death. The eulogy may thus serve as a vision and an imperative for growth. 4) to evoke the empathy and support of the community as an extended family for the family that is bereaved. In summary, the funeral process, though retaining its traditional form, is given new purpose, new meaning and new tasks. The end result is a compelling rite of passage capable of transforming the grieving family.

Woven into and following this presentation will be a description of the context in which this model has been applied, an evaluation of its benefits and liabilities in normative and problem situations, and a reflection on what this has meant to my ministry and may mean to the ministry of others. In the next sections, I will be laying out the theory according to its assumptions.

> If a man does away with his traditional way of living and throws away his good customs, he had better first make certain that he has something of value to replace them.
>
> *Basuto Proverb*

Grief And Family System

A death happens *in* a family. Families, like individuals, grieve. A family is a social system whose members relate to each other, interact with and are interdependent on each other in organized, predictable, repetitive patterns or sequences. As a social system, a family will tend to maintain equilibrium; there is a balance of tension which allows it to function and withstand stress and strain from the environment and from within the family.

In the normal family, this equilibrium gradually evolves and alters in response to aging and the changes in roles that life demands of its members. Typically, the most critical points of change are: courtship, marriage, parenthood, childhood, adolescence, recourtship and remarriage by "empty nesters", old age and death. It might be argued, then, that the family is an organism with its own life cycle and stages of development. And, as in the case of individual development, a family must attend to the tasks of one stage before it can adequately master the tasks of the next.

While there is invariably some stress and disorganization at each stage of the family life cycle, there is no stage as potentially threatening to family equilibrium as that of integrating the death of one of its members. The accustomed balance of roles is upset and out of kilter since the role of the deceased is not being played. Accustomed patterns of handling problems breakdown and are not effective in dealing with the stress and strain. And should the death occur at another critical point of change in the family life cycle, for example, at parenthood, at the marriage of a child or immediately following another death, the stress is even greater. The family system is in a state of chaos.

The disequilibrium into which a family is thrown by the death of one of its members may be considered the functional equivalent of grief in a family system; the process of adapting to the death is the counterpart of grief work or mourning. From the standpoint of the needs of the family system, the task is a achieve a new equilibrium through evolving new responses to social, economic and physical needs that were previously met by the one who has died. This process of accommodation occurs through processes of delegation, negotiation, repatterning and the utilization of outside resources.

In order for accommodation to be successful, there must be a balance between the needs of the family system as a whole and the developmental and personal needs of those making up the system. Otherwise, long-term family equilbrium will not occur. For example, if a girl in her early adolescence is co-opted to fill the roles of her deceased mother, is she also able to attend to the developmental tasks appropriate for one her age? Is she able to give sufficient time to her school work, to her peer group, to her fantasies? Even though her taking on the role of a parental child is presently working as an accommodation to the mother's death, what will happen over time? At what point will she reject the many impositions and the suppressing of her own needs? Whatever form this rejection may take — the equilibrium of the family will once again be threatened. The "grief work" of the family system is not complete.

Another way of looking at the effects of death on a family system is from the standpoint of personal grief work. A person's mourning can end when there is completion to the work of saying, doing, feeling and expressing whatever is there inside. At minimum, grief work depends upon the others in one's life giving permission to honor that which is seeking expression. Better still is the situation in which grief work is encouraged by others' empathy. Best of all is when the others' being empathic are one's own family.

Empathy is the capacity to feel as another does. It presupposes the other as a separate, unique being. No judgments are made about what the other should feel. As well as encouraging the other to express whatever feelings may exist, and for brief periods, to feel them as one's own, it is more than this. Empathy is a "personal making present" to oneself the other's total emotional and intellectual uniqueness — the lifetime of desires, feelings, thoughts and experiences that constitute the other's being. In making this real to oneself through imagination, one comes to understand the meaning of what the other is living.

When the members of bereaved families are able to respond to each other empathically, grief is apt to be expressed and fixation in the mourning process will be averted. When empathy is not present, however, grief is likely to remain unresolved, not only for individual family members but for the family system as well. The family may, for example, deny that a death has taken place and become fixated at what John Bowlby has called the first phase of mourning — "the urge to recover the lost object."[5] Among the ways in which a family may express its denial of death are: to remain silent regarding the death, to bring in a new family member to replace the one who has died, to maintain a "ghost" as part of the family (e.g., a deceased child's room that becomes a untouched shrine), or, through a family projection process, to endow a child with the characteristics of the deceased person. From this perspective, an acting out adolescent girl may ultimately be resisting her family's attempts to totally project her mother's characteristics upon her. This projection process, as well as the unresolved grief of which it is an expression, may be the evidence that this is a family in which empathy is wanting and the healthy expression of grief is unacceptable.

On the basis of perceptions such as this, Norman Paul has proposed the use of empathy in the resolution of grief work. What is unique to Paul is that he proposes that this be done in the context of family therapy. Paul writes:

> . . . fixation within the mourning process seems to be at the root of both individual psychopathology and a family's pathologically stable equilibrium . . . a connective grief experience, even though belated, seems to be the means for overcoming the fixation. A specific therapeutic technique has been developed that deliberately introduces a belated grief experience and emphasizes the elements of the mourning process . . .[6]

Paul's technique consists of empathizing with the resistance of the family members to experiencing and expressing the pain of grief even as he reviews the loss experience. By assuming an empathic stance, Paul models the behavior he is attempting to encourage. Family members are invited to show empathy as grief is expressed and to work through any resistance to observing others' grief reactions. The end result is reciprocal expressions of empathy that will lead to a reduction of family tensions, a sense of relief, and expressions of love towards each other.

Norman Paul's proposal for dealing with unresolved family grief is generally acknowledged as a classic among family therapists. Unfortunately, its very necessity reflects the failure of contemporary death rituals to address the needs of bereaved families. It also raises the question of how traditional society responds to these needs through its ritual processes. What are the characteristics of ritual process that address the family's need to grieve? How do they encourage grieving, evoke empathy and forestall family resistance? In answering these questions in the next section, we will also be in a position to reclaim those elements of ritual process that will permit our funerals to be more healing.

Ritual Process And Family Mourning

Ritual serves simultaneously to describe, legitimate and validate man's place in the cosmos and in society. It confers cosmic sanctions on social norms and validates man's understanding of the cosmic order through social practices. Ritual therefore simultaneously promotes equilibrium in society, its substystems (e.g., the family) and in the cosmos. Rites of passage, as ritual, serve these same functions in the case of individuals and families moving through their life cycles. Through participation in the processes of these rites, individuals and families are eased through stressful transitional periods to the end of affirming and maintaining personal, social and cosmic order.

Rites of passage are the transitional rituals accompanying changes of place, state, social position and age in a culture. In the case of bereavement, guidance through the funeral and mourning process takes the form of a rite of passage having a basically tripartite processual structure. This consists of three phases: 1) separation, 2) transition, margin or limen ("threshhold"), and 3) reintegration or reaggregation.

Separation rites detach the bereaved from their old places in society. Through rites of reintegration, their passage is consumated. Even as the mourners are likely to be going through psychological preparation for the post-mourning period during the time leading up to the final ceremony, at that ceremony they become publicly committed to finish with mourning. Often through rites of dropping the symbols of mourning, they are installed, inwardly transformed and possibly outwardly changed in roles and responsibilities, in their new places in society.

The predominant phase, however, is the liminal period, a transitional state and process of being "betwixt and between". The mourners are outside of conventional rites, roles and relations and bear few if any of the attributes of the past or coming state. They are stripped of status and authority, are removed from the social structure and are leveled to a homogeneous social state.

It is not surprising that the liminal phase should be likened to death, for it may be said that these practices mimic the death and transitional state of the one who had died. Such death-like behaviors constitute a social drama which remedies the mourners' sense of having a part of themselves die by dramatizing the situation itself.

Several features of the liminal phase that are integral to complete mourning and rebirth must be singled out in light of what is proposed below. The first of these is what Victor Turner calls "communitas"; the second is the reception of sacred knowledge.

Communitas is the sense of comradeship and communion that emerges among those jointly undergoing ritual transition. Evoked in the course of participating in the ritual process,

> The bonds of communitas are anti-structural in the sense that they are undifferentiated, equalitarian, direct, extant, nonrational, existential, I-Thou (in Feuerbach's and Buber's sense) relationships. Communitas is spontaneous, immediate, concrete - it is not shaped by norms, it is not institutionalized, it is not abstract . . . Structure, or all that which holds people apart, defines their differences, and constrains their actions, is one pole in a charged field, for which the opposite pole is communitas or anti-structure, the egalitarian "sentiment for humanity" of which David Hume speaks, representing the desire for a total, immediated relationship between person and person, a relationship which nevertheless does not submerge one in the other but safe-guards their uniqueness in the very act of realizing their commoness.[7]

For Turner, communitas is the primordial bond out of which all social structure emerges. It is experienced as something that is good, even pleasurable. There is something "magical" about it. "Subjectively there is in it the feeling of endless power."[8] Yet because communitas is spontaneous and immediate, it is short-lived. Yearning to preserve it, those who were bound together by it evolve an organized social system of norms and roles that may well last until death and in spite of any other distinctions of ascribed or achieved status.

Much of what is compelling and transformative in rites of passage is derived from communitas. In it, there is totality and presence, goodness and power and sense of the magical. It would not be an overstatement to say that communitas is compelling because it embodies and evokes a sense of the holy.[9]

What of the bereaved family in traditional society? How does this potential of communitas relate to it as it is ushered through the ritual of the funeral and mourning process? In light of what we know about grief and the functioning of family systems, it is likely that the agency of rebirth is found in the relational quality of communitas. The relational quality of communitas is strikingly similar to that of reciprocal empathy. In fact if they are compared, they are identical. What better mode of relation then, than that of communitas to nurture the expression of grief within a family system while simultaneously supporting and affirming the uniqueness of each family member. And how much more so, than when this is incorporated in a ritual process of stages and behaviors themselves appropriate to the duration and form of each stage of grieving?

The second feature of liminality that is integral to the mourning process is the transmitting of sacred knowledge to the mourner. What is communicated concerns the "ultimate things." It consists of complex semantic systems of pivotal, multivocal symbols, epics and myths. This may consist, for example, of the revelation of the real names, i.e., the essence, of the deities or presiding spirits. Central among these spirits are the spirits of one's ancestors, but especially the spirit of the one who has just died.

In traditional society, speech is not merely communication but also power and wisdom. The arcane knowledge or "gnosis" that is imparted has onto-logical value changing the inmost nature of the initiates. Sacred knowledge also has great conjunctive power. The text and context serve to bind the initiates together in a bond of communitas.[10]

As sacred knowledge is related to the bereaved family, it demands their full presence and attention by virtue of its urgency. Already moved towards communitas by isolation, the shared ordeal, common fears and a sense of shared destiny, sacred knowledge serves to confirm this mode of interaction. It infuses the setting and interactions with a sense of the holy and thereby with regenerating power.

The power of this sacred knowledge is, in part, a function of the ritual act or occasion itself, and the manner in which it is viewed by the initiate and the community. The event evokes great positive and negative feelings and is approached by all with the same trepidation and ambivalence with which one approaches the holy. As Otto has argued, the power of the sacred inheres in the mystery that is is simultaneously compelling and fascinating even while it evokes feelings of awe and dread.

One instance of this bipolar emotional valence is found in traditional puberty rites. The revelation of the secrets of sexuality, the promise of engaging in its pleasures, and the rights and privileges of adulthood are attractive and compelling. But there are also the dreaded ritual ordeals: circumcision, separation from mothers and a range of ascetic exercises. The initiate is forced to concentrate, to meditate; the ordeals make him vulnerable - open to instruction in the sacred values, beliefs and practices of the culture.

Death also partakes of this ambiguous, ambivalent quality of liminality. The dead, in particular, are associated with both positive and negative processes and objects. They decay - they are filthy, polluting and defiling. They punish and torment the living. And yet, if they are honored, they may bestow blessings. They are the powers that confer potency and fertility.

Their's is a mediating role. In preliterate society they are thought to mediate between the "invisible, ideal world of paradigms and archetypes and the sensorily perceptible world of sex and economics, begetting and food production, distribution and consumption."[11] In salvation religions, the dead participate in the drama of salvation -freeing or binding, punishing or rewarding the human soul. They are "the possessors of arcane knowledge, and prophecy or poetic inspiration (are) sought where the dead lie buried."[12]

In summary,

> the dead are conceived of as transformative agencies and as mediating between domains normally classified as distinct. These include the sensory as against the world of ideas, birth and death, structure and communitas, person and God, culture and nature . . . past and present . . .[13]

In the rituals surrounding death, as in all forms of initiation, there is a promise and hope. Whether literal or metaphorical, there is the possibility, in a sense, of communion with the dead—from prophets and heroes to the countless ordinary people present through the ages. In regarding them as part of a communitas that extends across time and space, they may be present to us as regenerating power and transforming grace.

Presence In Memory

Martin Buber has spoken of man's two primary attitudes or ways of being in relation to the world: I-Thou and I-It. The difference is not a function of the other but in the way one relates oneself to the other. I-Thou is characterized by mutuality, directness, presentness, intensity and ineffability. It is rare and momentary, and yet it is a basic human need for it is only within this relation that personality and the personal really exist. It is relation that is an end in itself, and in which there is authenticity, openness, and vulnerability. In I-Thou the other is seen and confirmed in his uniqueness. Empathy partakes of I-Thou relation. I-Thou is not limited to persons, but may include animals, trees, objects of nature, artistic creations, and God. Beyond this, I believe that when another has been met as Thou, even after that person has died, the memory of that presence abides as a potentiality that may be made present in our being.

I-It is the relationship of experiencing and using. It takes place within one, not between one and the other. It is entirely subjective and lacking in mutuality. It is the normative subject-object relationship in which the other is abstracted and is seen as a type or within a category. It is always mediate and indirect. It is significant only in connection and not in itself. In it there is safety since one has not exposed his vulnerability or authenticity. It is the normative relation, and in itself is neither good or bad. It is evil only when it is one's only relation, for if one lives only in the world of I-It, one is not a person — one is a thing. The It of I-It may equally well be a man, a woman, an animal, a being, a spirit, or a god.

Just as there are two relations to the world, there are two ways of remembering relation. There is It-memory. It is memory that is constituted of abstractions, concepts, qualities, categories, statistics, An It-memory may be of specific individual. This individual is reflected upon as an object of detached perception and experience. But this individual need not only have been experienced as an It. A person who was encountered as Thou may also be reflected upon as an It. Now, upon reflection, this person is experienced as an aggregate of qualities of which he seems to be constructed. Now we can place those qualities into a spatio-temporal-causal context within which each receives its place, its course, its measurability, its conditionality. It-memory is biography. To one who is so consigned, there is no presence.

There is also Thou-memory. It is memory in which a Thou is whole, unified, unique and dynamic in her presence. Thou-memory may also be of a particular person. This person is not only reflected upon, that is, experienced out of the past. In Thou-memory, the person is beheld in memory as a substance embracing all qualities, a potency that is active and effective in life. Thou-memory is an encounter with the past; it is epic. For one who is so remembered, there is a certain presence.

One who has died may be remembered in one or the other of these ways: in It-memory, or in Thou-memory. Though time and time again a Thou for me in life, and therefore having presence for me, the one whom I recall only in It-memory can no longer have presence. So remembered, my loved one remains lost for me in the Itness of death. But the Thouness of my loved one may also be redeemed from the Itness of death through the gracious gift of Thou-memory.

Thou-memory is an imagining and a making present even while it is a remembering. Remembrance presents in consciousness the image of my loved one encounterd as Thou. With my whole being, I intend the presence of this particular person through an act of imagining. The extent to which this imagining is met as a presence is an expression of the grace that emerges from the Eternal Presence. Buber writes:

> Our concern, our care must not be for the other side but for our own, not for grace but for will. Grace concerns us insofar as we proceed toward it and await its presence; it is not our object.[14]

As I will the Thouness of my loved one as a presence, I am affirming the Eternal Thou.

Thou-memory may also be the stuff of the "in-between". When Buber speaks of dialogue, he is not only providing a phenomenological description of man's two-fold attitude. He is also offering an ontology which points to the "in-between" as the really real. This sphere in which person meets person has generally been catalogued according to self and world, so that what happens to an individual is either an inner impression or an outer impression. Buber's point is that when two persons are *in relation* to each other, then there is an essential remainder which is common to them, but which reaches out beyond each. This remainder is the basic reality, the sphere of the in-between.[15]

Thou-memory may also be realized in the in-between of two persons meeting. I meet a person whose loved one has died. I listen as he speaks with meaning to me of the deceased. He remembers his loved one to me as a Thou in the most vital and powerful of ways: he relates a story of the deceased through a unity of tone, gesture, expression and word. I may respond in no less than four ways:

I can let his story die for want of an in-between. He has shared his remembrance with me as story, intending that I might meet his loved one. I do not will to take this up. I do not will to receive or affirm. Rather, I express perfunctory condolences, or wishing only to know what the deceased was, not who that person is in memory. I ask after the deceased as It: age, cause of death, number of survivors . . . It is not uncaring, this asking. But it is safe - as I stay within me. And so there is no in-between in which memory can become presence.

Or I may intend to become part of an event. I may will to make present the one who has died as this person, in memory, is to my friend. It is for me to will to encounter this person through a gift of imagining. Mine is an act of inclusion whereby I accept into myself the memory of relation with the deceased that is my friend's. As I intend the presence of the deceased through an imagining, I too may stand in relation with the deceased; yet the extent to which my imagining evokes a presence is an expression of grace. If it should be, it is an event of the in-between. In the poem "Do You Still Know It . . . . . ? Buber writes:

> Do you still know, how we in our young years
> Traveled together on this sea?
> Visions came, great and wonderful,
> We beheld them together, you and I.
> How image joined itself with images in our hearts!
> How a mutual animated describing
> Arose out of it and lived between thou and me!
> We were there and were yet wholly here
> And wholly together, roaming and grounded . . .[16]

I may also act to make the deceased present to Thou-memory for those who have *only* experienced him as an It. Now the task is one of moving these individuals to meet those who are present as Thous—especially those with whom there may already be a bond of trust, and in whom Thou-memory is potential or actual. Here the intention is one of linking and associating the ones of only It-memory to the deceased through the Thou-memory of those with whom encounter may be intended and realized.

Or I my intend otherwise - for my friend. Even as my friend relates his story I mean him as he is in his loss. I step into an elemental relation with him, intending the gift which Buber has called "imagining the real":

> a bold swinging—demanding the most intense stirring of one's being—into the life of the other. This is the nature of all genuine imagining, only that here the realm of my action is not the all - possible, but the particular real person who confronts me, whom I can attempt to make present to myself just in this way, and not otherwise . . . Let it be said again that all this can only take place in a living partnership, that is, when I stand in a common situation with the other and expose myself vitally to his share in the situation as really his share.[16]

In making present this person confronting me, I encounter his own intending. In turning to my friend as he is, I receive him as my partner and, to the extent it is possible, I confirm and affirm his own intending of his loved one's presence. Intention is joined with intention - even so, we still must await grace. Should it be bestowed, then my friend is realized as the I of I-Thou—memory.

Just as man's primary attitude is two-fold, so is the I of man; the I of I-Thou is different from the I of I-It. The I of I-It appears as an ego conscious of itself as a subject of experience and use. This I appears by setting itself apart from others in order to experience and use. Buber writes that the purpose of this "is living , which means dying one human life long."[18] For this I there is no participation and no actuality; this I has only a past and no present. His dynamics are setting himself apart and taking possession—and the object is always It, that which is not actual.

The I of I-Thou appears as a person conscious of himself as subjectivity. This I appears by entering into relation to other persons. The purpose of this relation is the relation itself - touching the Thou. This I, standing in relation, participates in an actuality and is thereby actual. As person, the I of I-Thou becomes conscious of himself as participating in being, as being - with, and thus as a being. This person beholds his self.

One may also be the I of I-It - memory or the I of I-Thou-memory. As one whose loved one had died, the I of I-It-memory is an ego turned inward, occupying itself with its missing object. The possessions which were the deceased—the tasks she performed and the hungers she satisfied for me, the responsibilities of which she relieved me, the utility she was to me—all these I miss. And so I seek them in the void, the past - only, the Itness of death. Without center and way for my grief, I turn ever more inward, finding even more the Itness of the void within. But perhaps I shall meet one who in offering Thou-memory to me will have offered me the center and the way.

The nature of a Thou is that is comes into being only in relation: "Relation is reciprocity. My You acts on me as I act on it."[19] Mutuality is also found in relation, though its completeness is defined by whether one partner is acting on the other so as to accomplish some goal. Reciprocity and mutuality are also true of my I in relation to Thou-memory.

Perhaps it was with something of this in mind that Buber composed the following, dedicated to the memory of his beloved son-in-law Ludwig Strauss—a commentary on the Ḧolderlin verse "Since We Have Been Dialogue":

> In the measure that each of us reveals himself to the others, fulfilling the speech that he is, we allow the Coming One to come until out of the ability to hear that characterizes existence in reciprocity, "all experience one another" and so in the renewed "silence" in the "evening of time" there is again "a speech among the living" and the pure voices resound together, no longer a dialogue but "a chorus now", the dead with the living, hence "all mortals whom we know until now", "all one in you", in "the God of gods", who uttered and heard them have dialogue with the gods, the messengers to whom he is God.[20]

My loved one has died. But though she is physically absent,her presence as my Thou-in-memory makes of my I her Thou. As there is presence for her in memory, so there is a certain presence for me. As she has become a personlikeness, so I become a person. And just as the Thouness of my beloved has been redeemed from the Itness of death, so I am able to turn back to life. Knowing her presence in memory, I am able to accept her absence in death. Death is not wholly It. Within it there glimmers the potentiality of presence.

Out of our meeting has come the possibility of accepting the reality of death, a being present to the world around me and an awareness of my being a person. The possibility of relation itself has also been affirmed. And so the way is open for my turning to others to empathize, to grieve, indeed to intend the memory of the Thou that may now be absent to them.

But there is more. Because of the character of relation, I also transcend myself: "Human life touches upon absoluteness," and acquires "absolute meaning" that surpasses its "own conditioned nature."[21]

Relation brings man into the "between man and God," for God is the Eternal Thou in whom the extended lines of relation meet. "Every single You is a glimpse of that. Through every single You the basic word addresses the eternal You."[23] As I intend the presence of my loved one in Thou-memory, I am affirming the Eternal Thou. In this affirmation, there is the possibility of response.

Buber maintains that there are personal experiences related to the revelatory experiences recorded in sacred texts. We may suddenly and unexpectedly become aware of a certain apperception now present within ourselves but that was lacking just a moment ago. Unable to discover its origin, we realize that what happened to us is "otherness." We know it is a gift graciously bestowed by a source outside ourselves. It is not something produced out of our own unconscious and that was latent in the depths of our soul.

While my Thou-memory may be the agency for this experience, it is not the source. For this presence, like the presence of all things, inheres in God's Eternal Presence. Through encountering the Thou of my loved one in memory, I may receive a semblance of that which, according to Buber, man receives in revelation:

> Man receives, and what he receives is not a "content" but a presence as strength. This presence and strength includes three elements that are not separate but may nevertheless be contemplated as three. First, the whole abundance of actual reciprocity, of being admitted, of being associated while one is altogether unable to indicate what that is like with which one is associated . . . and this is second: the inexpressible confirmation of meaning. It is guaranteed. Nothing, nothing can henceforth be meaningless . . . This comes third: it is not the meaning of "another life" but that of this our life . . . and it wants to be demonstrated by us in this world. The meaning can be received but not experienced; it cannot be experienced, but it can be done; and this is what it intends with us. The guarantee does not wish to remain shut up within me, it wants to be born into the world by me.[24]

Evoking A Presence In Light Of Ritual Theory

Victor Turner would classify what I have received as sacred knowledge. Among its characteristics, sacred knowledge has conjunctive power. So, too, through standing in relation with Thou-memory, I have received a sense of relatedness that seeks expression in bondedness with those about me. This is the stuff of communitas. In fact, Turner maintains that:

> Communitas rests on Buber's I-Thou and "essential We". Extreme individualism only understands a part of man. Extreme collectivism only understands man as a part. Communitas is the implicit law of wholeness arising out of relations between totalities.[25]

Buber speaks of the "essential We" as an attitude of community living. It is that mode of relation at the group level which corresponds to I-Thou relation at the level of dyads. The "essential We" only comes about when independent people have come together in essential relation and directness in moving towards a freely chosen common goal. It includes the Thou potentially, for "only men who are capable of truly saying Thou to one another can truly say We with one another."[26]

A family member has died. The survivors intend the presence in memory of the Thou they shared in life; now this memory is the common center and a common bond. As this presence is realized, each, in turn, is made present as the I of I-Thou-memory. Turning to the others so graced, each is capable of speaking the primary word I-Thou, and thereby may act to speak the family system as a We that is communitas. Consider how much greater this potential, should one within or coming to the family turn to the others, receive them as partners, affirm them in intending the presence of their loved one in Thou-memory and encourage them to do the same for each other. Bestowed this gift, the family will move to accept the reality of death, speak with directness, trust and confide in each other and share reciprocal empathy. The process of grieving and of renegotiating family rules and responsibilities may then proceed, resting on a sound emotional and relational foundation. There is relatedness. There is meaning to life. There is an imperative to live.

Turner would draw other parallels in classifying what may be received in Thou -memory as a type of the sacred knowledge conveyed in liminality. There is a presence and a sense of power to both. Turner, in fact, makes it a point that the dead are especially associated with power—both negative (that inherent in punishment and defilement) and positive (that conferring potency and fertility).[27] Moreover, the entire experience of "flow", the merging of action and awareness in liminality, and associated with the receiving of sacred knowledge, is synonymous with "presence".[28]

Sacred knowledge concerns the "ultimate things". As knowledge of these things is communicated, their ontological value is such that the inmost nature of the initiates may be transformed. In preliterate societies, frequently what is communicated concerns the realm of the dead—particularly their secret, *real* names by which they might be invoked. Because one who knows these names knows the essence of the spirits themselves, this person, so initiated, is able to *invoke* their *presence at will.* This same structure is manifest in the act of *intending to evoke* the deceased's *presence* in Thou -memory. Ours is the modern day analogue to this ancient practice. Moreover, it is capable of effecting the same sense of transformation.

Finally, Turner writes of the spirits of the dead serving a mediating function between the various domains and dimensions of the world. In our model, the memory of the deceased as Thou plays the same role. It is the common center of "goal" about which a family system may constellate as a communitas or "essential We". It may also be the agency for grace through which I might stand in I - Thou relation and realize presence, wholeness and personhood. Finally, it may be the vehicle of quasi-revelatory experience and of a sense of standing in relation with God.

From the standpoint of ritual theory, evoking a presence in Thou - memory among the members of a bereaved family would address many of the needs to which funeral and mourning rites traditionally responded. It fosters a bondedness and modesty of interaction conducive to the expression of grief and the renegotiation of roles and rules; both of these are essential for a return to a functional family equilibrium. It also confirms the reality of the death while at the same time conveys a sense of life's meaningfulness. God is met as a Presence that confers meaning even as this presence urges man's response.

Supporting Evidence

There is a body of evidence that supports our theory of the efficacy of evoking a presence. This evidence takes both conceptual and empirical form. A number of pastoral and secular thinkers have explanations of the psychodynamics of grief that would justify the pragmatics of our approach.

In *Mourning and Melancholia,* for example, Freud suggested that grief is a process by which a person progressively withdraws the energy that ties him or her to the loved object:

> This energy was conceived by Freud as being bound to the memories and ideas that arose from interaction with the dead person. To become free of his tie to this person, the energy has to be detached by a process that Freud termed "hypercathexis," a process that requires the mourner to turn his back on the real world, and to invest free energy in the struggle to "decathect" the loved object. By focusing his mind on the lost person and bringing to consciousness each relevant memory, the mourner gradually sets free the bound up energy.

As well as accounting for the value of our approach, this view is consistent with two observations. First, those who are recently bereaved often obsess over memories of the dead person. Second, they spend a great deal of time reliving the events leading up to the death. Freud's theory also suggests a more positive outcome for the bereaved person who faces up to the loss than for one who avoids thinking about it. These observations, in turn, are consistent with the data.

Others have offered explanations equally supportive of our proposal. Switzer, for example, points out that: "One's self has certain aspects of the life of the significant other as a living component of it. When the other dies, the self is perceived as threatened with death by the loss of the other."[30] From this perspective, one can redeem the situation by reaffirming the other which is within one as living as a part of one's self. Abraham speaks of this as a reaction to object loss by setting up the object within one's own ego through introjection. The psychological result is: "my loved object is not gone, for I now carry it within myself and can never lose it."[31] Finally, Oates refers to the psychological "death, burial and resurrection of . . . selfhood in the process of grief."[32] When the introjection of the other is understood to be alive within the self, the self becomes whole and fully alive again.

There are also solid empirical findings that support our approach. Most especially, Glick, *et al.* report that in their study of bereaved widows, the majority seemed comforted by immersion in memories of their husband. In addition, almost all widows reported repeated experiences of feeling their husband was just about to arrive home or was with them. Many reported a relatively steady sense of this presence. In contrast to most other aspects of loss, the sense of the persisting presence of the husband did not diminish with time. Once established, it seemed as likely to be reported late in bereavement as early. The authors account for this in the following manner:

> Perhaps one explanation for the persistence of the sense of the husband's presence was that it was comforting rather than disturbing. Many widows reported that they deliberately invoked it when they were especially unsure or depressed - it made

them feel less alone. They did not generally feel uneasy about having this sense of the husband's presence unless they also had other grounds for concern about their emotional stability.[33]

Conclusions And Implications

The central concern of this project has been to offer clergy a model of the funeral that maximizes its value given the attenuated ritual approach to mourning in our society. I have argued the need to attend to the needs of the grieving family system. This is because the family system is an organism in its own right and has its own tasks to perform in evolving a new, functional equilibrium. I am also offering this model because the family system is the primary source of support or sabotage for grieving individuals. Finally, this project has relied upon ritual theory as the standard for evaluating what is most compelling in traditional renewal and mourning rites. The resulting theory and its application are based, in good part, on the philosophy of Martin Buber. This is because its emphasis on relation permits an equally positive interface with family systems theory and with ritual theory. More important than this, it disposes to a theory and practice generalized to most denominational settings. Finally, much of what is integral to my own thinking has been shaped by Buber's emphasis on God as Presence/Eternal Thou, and on the I-Thou attitude. The central feature of what is proposed here—the idea of evoking the presence of the deceased in Thou-memory—is offered in light of these considerations.

Translated into practical terms, I envision the following: The contact clergy have with bereaved family systems is frequently limited to a prefuneral meeting and to the funeral and burial service. The intention in the former is to elicit the sharing of stories about the deceased as a Thou in order to intend the presence of the Thou in the memory of family members as well as for me. The intention is one of redeeming Thouness, not of fabricating a therapy. If realized through grace, virtually all of the other values will follow in turn: communitas, empathy, presence, negotiation, power and meaning. In addition, information is communicated that may be incorporated into the eulogy. The eulogy is offered as an act of making present—as an affirmation of the family's intending of presence, and of their emergence as an "essential We" or communitas. Finally, the eulogy is intended as well to evoke the empathic response of the congregation and of the wider community. The specific tasks and considerations in implementing this model, and the related issues of context, evaluation and reflection will be discussed in sections on applying the theory to the pre-funeral meeting and the development of the eulogy for congregational celebration.

1. Ira D. Glick, Robert S. Weiss, and C. Murray Parkes, *The First Year of Bereavement* (New York: John Wiley & Sons, 1974), pp. 97-117.
2. Paul C. Rosenblatt, Patricia R. Walsh, and Douglas A. Jackson, *Grief and Mourning in Cross-Cultural Perspective* (Human Relations Area Files Press, 1976) p. 96.
3. Robert L. Moore et al., "Symposium on Ritual in Human Adaptation," *Zygon* 18 (September 1983): 209.
4. Edgar Jackson, *The Christian Funeral: Its Meaning, Its Purpose, and Its Modern Practice* (New York: Channel Press, 1966); Paul Irion, *The Funeral and the Mourners: Pastoral Care of the Bereaved* (Nashville: Abingdon Press, 1966); Jack Bloom, "The Eulogy as a Tool in Grief Work," *Pastoral Psychology* (December 1970; reprint ed.); Dave McMahill, "The

Funeral Service as a Ministry of Meanings," *Aging and the Human Spirit,* ed. Carol LeFevre and Perry LeFevre (Chicago: Exploration Press, 1981).
5. John Bowlby, "Processes of Mourning," *International Journal of Psychoanalysis* 42:317-340.
6. Normal L. Paul, "The Use of Empathy in the Resolution of Grief," *Perspectives in Biology and Medicine* 11 (Autumn 1967): 162-63.
7. Victor Turner, *Dramas, Fields, and Metaphors* (Ithaca: Cornell University Press, 1974), p. 274.
8. *Idem, The Ritual Process* (Ithaca: Cornell University Press, 1969), p. 139.
9. *Ibid.*, pp. 96-97.
10. *Ibid.*, p. 103; Turner, *Dramas,* p. 259.
11. Victor Turner, *Process, Performance and Pilgrimage* (New Delhi: Concept Publishing, 1979), p. 127.
12. Mircea Eliade, *Rites and Symbols of Initiation,* trans. Willard R. Trask (New York: Harper Torchbooks, 1965), p. 37.
13. Turner, *Process,* p. 142.
14. Martin Buber, *I and Thou,* trans. Walter Kaufman (New York: Charles Scribner's Sons, 1970) p. 124.
15. *Idem, Between Man and Man,* trans. Ronald Gregor Smith (Boston: Beacon Press, 1955) pp. 202-05.
16. *Idem, A Believing Humanism: Gleanings,* ed. Ruth Nanda Anshen, trans. Maurice Friedman (New York: Simon and Schuster, 1967), p. 51.
17. *Idem, The Knowledge of Man,* ed. Maurice Friedman trans. Maurice Friedman and Ronald Gregor Smith (New York: Harper Torchbooks, 1965), p. 18.
18. *Idem, I,* p. 112.
20. *Idem, Believing,* pp. 85-6.
21. *Idem, Between,* pp. 168, 167.
22. *Idem, I,* p. 113.
23. *Ibid.*, p. 123.
24. *Ibid.*, pp. 158-59.
25. Turner, *Process,* p. 75.
26. Buber, *Between,* pp. 175 ff.
27. Turner, *Process,* pp. 125 ff.
28. *Ibid.*, p. 55 ff.
29. Glick, p. 6.
30. David K. Switzer, *The Dynamics of Grief* (Nashville: Abingdom Press, 1970), p. 200.
31. *Ibid.*, pp. 200-01.
32. *Ibid.*, p. 201.
33. Glick, p. 147.

CHAPTER II

Discerning Religious Meaning in the Divorce Adjustment Process

BY ROBERT HURST

INTRODUCTION

Pastors increasingly are called upon to counsel with persons adjusting to marital separation and divorce. Much of the secular work in the field has tended toward "support group" counseling approaches. These methods implicitly or explicitly have understood divorce adjustment as a grief process.[1] The pastoral counseling literature in the field has also concentrated on the themes of grief and loss. Pastors are familiar with grief conceptualized as a "process," and divorce adjustment shares some points in common with grief. In divorce, however, personal responsibility for the loss incurred is often more immediate and direct, than in other forms of loss. Further, since approximately 75% of divorced women and 80% of divorced men remarry,[2] divorce adjustment counseling must also be concerned with preparation for new intimacy. For these reasons, I believe the "grief process model" is not adequate for divorce adjustment counseling.

Over the past four years I have worked with approximately fifty persons adjusting to divorce. Several cases I have had the opportunity to follow over an extended period of time, two years and more. I have observed that the emotional dislocation of divorce prompts many persons to question their assumptions about the meaning and purpose of life. Persons adjusting to divorce often experience a new openness to prayer and an increased awareness of the presence of sin in their lives as a result of marital failure. This heightened self-reflection offers opportunities for growth in relationship to God. Much of my counseling with the divorced, then, has consisted in offering direction in their spiritual development, helping them to interpret their experience in religious terms. I have further observed that the process of adjusting to a divorce can be facilitated by growth in the spiritual life, suggesting that offering spiritual direction can be a valid approach in ministering to divorced persons.

Therefore, I have formulated a model of divorce adjustment which draws upon traditional concepts of spiritual direction: confession, repentance, forgiveness. This model can be helpful to pastors in four ways: 1. Founded on the concepts of confession, repentance and forgiveness the model is grounded in the tradition of the church. 2. Defining divorce adjustment in terms of spiritual tasks empowers the pastor to make intervention as a spiritual director. 3. The use of "repentance" strongly emphasizes the need for personal transformation in preparation for new intimacy. 4. The model does not require regular weekly counseling sessions, a benefit to the pastor's schedule.

The paper will begin by offering a theoretical model of divorce adjustment in terms of spiritual direction. The rest of the paper will then offer illustrative material from the personal journal of a case study who will be referred to as "J".[3]

The Model

The divorce adjustment process can be understood in terms of three traditional categories of spiritual direction: confession, repentance and forgiveness. These three categories can be divided into ten cycles (see figure 1): confession consisting of five cycles, repentance three, forgiveness two. The key to movement from one cycle to the next is the accomplishment of spiritual tasks (see figure1).[4] These tasks spiritually define the changes in thinking and feeling which occur as persons move through the adjustment process.

The movement from one cycle to the next is not always clearly discernible. The cycles overlap. Over time there is progress as persons move through confession to repentance and forgiveness. Frequent regression is common. Becoming acquainted with some forms of thinking and emotional expression which accompany these cycles can help the pastor to develop a general sense of where a counselee may be in the adjustment process. Then with knowledge of the spiritual task or tasks confronting the individual, the pastor can offer direction. Remembering that each cycle does not always flow neatly and in the "proper" order, a description of the process is now offered.

Figure I

The Divorce Adjustment Process

Confession:

Cycle One: Denial

Spiritual Tasks: Moving from nostalgia toward hope, moving from denial of loss toward facing the end of the relationship.

Cycle Two: Blaming Others

Spiritual Task: Moving from protestations of innocence toward admission of guilt.

Cycle Three: Blaming Self

Spiritual Task: Moving from using guilt feelings to evade change of behavior toward attending to the task of changing behavior.

Cycle Four: Responsibility

Spiritual Tasks: Moving from nostalgia toward hope, moving from evading responsibility toward assuming responsibility.

Cycle Five: Acceptance.

Spiritual Task: Moving from the denial of loss toward accepting the end of the relationship.

Repentance:

Cycle One: Turning Around

Spiritual Task: Discerning the presence of false consciousness or sin, and imaging truth.

Cycle Two: Insight

Spiritual Task: Identifying specific behaviors resulting from false consciousness or sin, and imaging change.

Cycle Three: Will

Spiritual Task: Moving away from sin, false consciousness, toward truth by changing behavior.

Forgiveness:

Cycle One: Integration

Spiritual Task: Reconciliation.

Cycle Two: New Intimacy

Spiritual Task: Faith

Confession

Cycle One: Denial

The first cycle of confession is denial. To express their thoughts many people use phrases like, "I can't believe it is happening," or "it is all so unreal." Emotional expressions are full of shock, confusion and disbelief. These are essentially defense mechanisms which help the person to "buy time," so that the fear and emotional dislocation can be experienced a little at a time. The first spiritual task in this first cycle is to move away from nostalgia toward hope. The principal reason for denial in the beginning is that the only hope appears to be in the past, rather than the future. The second spiritual task is to move away from the denial of loss toward a facing of the end of the relationship. Any facing of loss will bring the counselee in touch with the fear for survival in the face of the prospective catastrophe of breaking up their home. Life will never be the same. Shared possessions and children must be split-up or lost. Life styles must change, because the family income will have to support two households.

If the person has some sort of prayer life or is at least comfortable with prayer, an intervention can be made to help a move away from nostalgia toward hope. Very simply an individual can focus his or her prayers on the future, honestly confessing fear and trusting God's providence. The more the individual seeks hope in the future, the less he or she will be tied to the past, thus enabling movement toward the facing of the end of the relationship.

An important note should be made before continuing. Many counselees will come long after the denial cycle is over. For many persons, especially those initiating the divorce, the cycle of denial may have occurred over several years as a process of deliberation concerning whether or not they should stay in the marriage. Thus, denial may have been confronted as part of marriage counseling leading up to separation or divorce.

Cycle Two: Blaming Others

The second and third cycles of confession can be interchangeable depending upon the individual. Both cycles focus on blaming. Those who initiate a divorce/separation express much of their anger in their leaving. They tend to begin the blaming process with themselves. The spouses who do not initiate divorce/separation tend to experience themselves as "victims" and begin in cycle two blaming the other spouse.

Cycle two can be understood as a continuation of cycle one. "It was all his/her fault," is another way of denying reality. Unconsciously the counselee is saying, "I can't believe this is happening, because I can't think of anything I did to cause it, therefore, it must be all his/her fault." Many people become "stuck" in this cycle. The spiritual task of moving away from protesting innocence toward an admission of guilt will help the person to move. The key, however, to enabling this movement is to facilitate the expression of anger.

The irrational need to blame an ex-spouse for the failure of marriage is usually rooted in a deep well of unexpressed anger. The counselee will continue to remain stuck blaming the ex-spouse until their anger is expressed. Many people experience difficulty expressing their anger directly, because they have been taught that anger is sinful. This is a religious pathology with turns anger into hate and hostility, and also leads to the self-righteous perfectionism which supports the protestations of innocence in this cycle. A pastor in the role of spiritual director in such cases can be particularly effective in "giving permission" for the expression of anger. Good scriptural authority can be found in Ephesians 4: 25-27.

Cycle Three: Blaming Self

After an individual expresses his/her anger and lets go of the need to protest his/her innocence, the realization of the counselee's own guilt often comes rushing in with thoughts like, "it was all my fault." The feelings in this cycle are guilt, shame, depression. The relative healthiness of a person's reaction to this cycle depends upon the ability to experience guilt as an assumption of responsibility pointing toward hope in the future, rather than an affixing of blame which looks nostalgically to the past. Thus, the working out of the spiritual task, moving from using guilt feelings to evade change of behavior toward attending to the task of changing in the future, is critical. If someone becomes stuck, an offering of absolution by the pastor and the announcement of forgiveness can help a move through this cycle. If the counselee persists in feeling guilty he/she can be challenged in two ways. First, "if God has forgiven your past actions, why can't you forgive yourself? Are you placing yourself above God?" Often people remain stuck in guilt because they are too proud to accept forgiveness. The second question which must be asked when guilt persists is "how is your guilt preventing you from changing?" Here the person may need to be confronted with the insight of the pastor, that persistent guilt is a way of not letting go of the past and avoidance of change.

Cycle Four: Responsibility

The spiritual task of cycle four focuses upon moving away from evading responsibility toward owning a mutual responsibility for the break-down of the marriage. Some of the changes in thinking in this cycle involve realizing that many of the problems in the marital relationship had deep roots in the past of the individual partners and were brought into the marriage, rather than having been caused by the marriage. In addition in this cycle counselees often realize that the "misbehaviors" which many times lead up to the marital break-up are part of a pattern of behavior forming an intricate dance by which the partners generate the emotional energy for divorce and share responsibility for ending the marriage.[5]

As the individual develops in his/her appreciation of mutual responsibility for the end of the marriage, a danger of regression develops. There is a reawakening of nostalgia, "if only I had known that before, things could have been different." Emotionally a desire may develop to bargain prematurely with the ex-spouse for a resumption of the relationship. Here the pastor can emphasize the spiritual task of moving away from nostalgia toward hope in the future. It is possible a couple may achieve a reconciliation in the future, the pastor may encourage this hope, but if there is an hope, it is not in a resumption of the old relationship. Until both parties have moved through the cycles of repentance they are not prepared to form a new relationship.

Cycle Five: Finishing the Past

As the counselee moves away from the nostalgia of the past to hope in the future, he/she will move toward the feeling of acceptance of the end of the relationship. The spiritual task of the fifth cycle of confession is to move away from the denial of loss toward accepting the end of the relationship. The fifth cycle of confession, however, is deceptive. At this point it is true the past is finished. However, the pastor must fight the idea that the individual is finished, for the work of repentance is only beginning. The danger is that the person, emotionally free of the past relationship will seek to remarry before he/she has fully worked through the personality problems which tormented the previous marriage. One way of confronting the dilemma is to say: "The past now is finished. But you are not. Now we work on the future."

Repentance

Cycle One: Turning Around

The first tentative stirrings of repentance can be found, when the counselee works on the spiritual task of moving from protestations of innocence toward admission of guilt. As the person moves more toward looking for hope in the future, repentance emerges with thoughts like: "I need to change." "The future won't be different until I change." The spiritual task in this first cycle of repentance is to move toward discerning false consciousness or sin within the life-style of the individual. The discipline of Adlerian Life-Style Analysis can be a useful tool in this cycle of repentance, because it helps to link present problems to broad behavior patterns which grow out of childhood conditioning. One of the goals implicit in this spiritual task is to help the counselee to understand that sin is not a mere behavior attached to an otherwise healthy personality. Sin is a false consciousness, a misapprehension of reality which forms part of a person's identity. To initiate change at this level is to become a new person. Emotionally, in this cycle of turning around, the counselee is likely to express wonder and determination—revelation. It is as if the veil has been parted.

Cycle Two: Insight

The spiritual task of cycle two of repentance is for the counselee to identify specific behaviors resulting from false consciousness and imagine change. This does not mean sitting around day dreaming about the perfect self. Instead, the counselee must identify specific actions which grow out of the broad behavior patterns identified in cycle one of repentance, and make specific plans to behave differently.

As the individual increases in his/her understanding of the relationship between suffering and the inadequacies of his/her life style he/she emotionally experiences encouragement. The thought begins to grow: "I can be different," which captures the awakening sense that the individual is no longer a victim.

Cycle Three: Will

In the third cycle of repentance the spiritual task is to get on with the hard business of changing self by changing behavior. Repentance may have seemed easy until this point. Now devotion and discipline are required and regression is common. The counselee needs patience; the pastor can offer encouragement. The individual may struggle in this cycle for weeks, months, even years. This is the hard effort of practicing virtue until it becomes integrated into the personality. The pastor as spiritual director can help the counselee to design creatively appropriate penitential disciplines. As change occurs emotionally hopefulness increases; the thought begins to grow: "the future can be different."

Forgiveness

Cycle One: Intergration

As the counselee begins to pull together the pieces of his or her life, a feeling of wholeness begins to emerge. A concept of forgiveness at a newer and deeper level is expressed—"I am a new person." This forgiveness is more than a release from past guilt, it is a sensing of grace by which the individual has been transformed. The spiritual task of the first cycle of forgiveness is reconciliation, a pulling together of fragments and the recognition of new wholeness. Here some "ritual of integration" may help the counselee to "finish." One woman with whom I worked invited her friends to a special worship service during which she thanked them for all the help and love they had extended to her; she publicly reaffirmed her baptismal vows, and we celebrated communion. Each person will have his/her own way of "finishing." The pastor may be of assistance in providing a ritual context for this expression.

Cycle Two: New Intimacy

Finally, the individual is ready for new intimacy. The spiritual task is faith, venturing out into an imperfect world and seeking to relate intimately with other human beings. If somehow this task is not accomplished, or at least attempted, then forgiveness has not been realized. This cycle may or may not involve remarriage or even new sexual relationships, but the person in a new way is prepared to love.

A Case Study "J"

Introduction

"J" began her journal August 14, 1978. On September 1, 1978 she asked her husband for a divorce. A brief attempt at marital counseling was tried. On September 30, 1978 "J" and her husband contacted an attorney to arrange a divorce. The last week of October 1978 "J" began attending a ten week divorce adjustment seminar led by my wife Beth and me. "J" 's spouse moved out the first week in November, and their divorce was final the end of that month.[6]

My first contact with "J" came when she enrolled in the divorce adjustment seminar. During the ten weeks of the seminar the participants were encouraged to review their "stories " as part of the process of moving toward an understanding of mutual responsibility for their divorces. In addition many practical problems of adjusting to single life were discussed. "J" consulted with me privately on three occasions during the ten weeks of the seminar. These interviews focused on her feelings of guilt and anger. Using the gestalt two chair dialogue technique, I helped "J" to express her feelings. When she expressed guilt because she felt angry, I offered the insight from Ephesians 4: 25-27 that anger only becomes sinful if it is unexpressed and becomes part of wall of resentment between two persons. When "J" continued to hang on to her feelings of guilt concerning actions in the past, I offered her absolution, which assisted her in moving toward future oriented change.

After the divorce adjustment seminar "J" began attending infrequently the church of which I was the pastor. She consulted with me on an irregular basis for about one and a half years. Her first contacts after the seminar concerned her new dating relationships. She felt shame about her sexual encounters with men. She seemed overly concerned about the opinion of others about her behavior. I encouraged her to learn to exercise her own judgement and stop worrying about what "Others may think." After some "experimentation" "J" on her own initiative began to change her relationships with men.

During Lent of 1979 "J" consulted with me concerning her prayer life. I encouraged her to adopt a regular discipline of self-reflection and meditation as part of her prayers. Also I urged her to adopt a penitential discipline of giving up going to a local tavern. These spiritual exercises helped "J" to seek more stable relationships with men and reflect upon those aspects of her personality which impeded the development of intimacy.

After March of 1979 my contacts with "J" were irregular and focused primarily upon her struggle to relate intimately with men. This was "repentance" work. Regression was frequent. My principal interventions were to offer encouragement and insight in four areas: 1. To love another, one must love self; "J" needed to develop a more positive self-image. 2. Intimate relationships without friendship are empty and meaningless; "J" needed to move away from the "instant intimacy" of casual sex and work toward the deeper and more difficult spiritual intimacy which accompanies friendship. 3. Friendship is founded upon an honest expression of feeling; "J" needed to move away from her obsession with pleasing and appeasing men toward honestly expressing her thoughts and feelings. 4. Life must be lived in the here and now; "J" needed to move away from fantasizing how she hoped her relationships would result in marriage toward working on her relationships in the present moment.

In the Spring of 1980 a significant pastoral intervention helped "J" begin to move through repentance toward forgiveness. "J" participated in a weekend retreat led by me February 29—March 2 of 1980. Several gestalt therapy techniques were used. At one point using a fantasy exercise "J" was exploring an empty feeling in her chest. When she fantasized going inside her body to explore the feeling, it appeared to her to be a dark empty room. As she explored further, she found the room only had three walls, and the group encouraged her to walk in the direction where there was no wall. As she proceeded she found a bright glowing light which surrounded and warmed her. She took the light back to the empty room and looked around. Then she said, "I think maybe I can start to fill this room again."

When I talked with "J" about this experience later, she said, "In that light I found the Lord." After this experience "J" reported increased feelings of internal peace.

In May of 1980 "J" came to me, because she felt she had lost the feeling of peace which had grown out of her retreat experience. In conversation she identified that the peace had left her when she had become sexually involved with a new boy friend. I offered the insight that she was experiencing alienation in her relationship with God because she was idolizing her new boy friend. By trying to please and appease her new lover, she had forsaken the honest expression of her own thoughts and feelings. She had fallen back into her basically negative self-image which set men on a pedestal in the place of God. As "J" worked with this insight, she determined to change her behavior and insist upon honesty and committment in relationship rather than casual sex. When she began to put her resolve into action, "J" reported that her prayer life improved and the feeling of peace returned.

In May of 1980 "J" began attending worship regularly as well as helping with several church projects. Over the one and a half year period from November 1979 to June of 1980 I spent approximately one and a half hours per month with "J", including some contacts in group situations as well as private interviews.

Confession

Evidence exists that "J" had been feeling dissatisfaction in her marriage for several years, and three and half months prior to beginning her journal had begun pondering whether or not to remain faithful to the marriage, when on a chance meeting she became infatuated with another man. She began writing as an exercise to help sort out the confusion of denial:

> *No way to express clearly and accurately how I'm feeling now. I'll try though, thinking it may help. (8/14/78)*

"J" 's thinking in the beginning of her journal was filled with denial. She recognized there was a problem but then attempted to dismiss its importance:

> *Sounds like the typical loss of excitement—itchy—stage every marriage goes through to me. Many make it through it. That gives me heart. . . . I find it surprising that I don't want to stay married. Disappointed that I probably will be there in this marriage in the future. It's like I want out. I guess it goes as part of wanting to be independent. . . . I feel when I get "Me" together and feeling productive again, that the pendulum will once again bring my feelings back to a happy medium concerning Jx* (the spouse). *(8/14/78)*

In the case of "J" instances of denial in her thinking and her emotional expression persisted during the separation, divorce and afterward for about a year. The persistence of denial is common in divorce adjustment especially during times of stress and transition. The following examples help to illustrate:

> *So today I called the Lawyer but was unable to get an appointment until Monday. I still can't believe we're going through with it. (9/30/78)*
>
> *It's spooky like I'm in a dream world—or freaking out. Maybe I am crazy. . . . If it weren't that I was scared and in doubt about finding a good job to support the children, I'd be tickled pink about this whole thing. (10/12/78)*

Then at times nostalgia hits me—a look outside at the backyard and spring and thoughts of all the springs Jx (ex-spouse) *and I had together. Really makes me sick. Wow! What have I done? (4/2/79)*

"J" began the spiritual task of cycle one—moving from nostalgia towards hope— about three months before beginning her journel. She did this by developing an infatuation with another man with whom she fantasized a love affair. In my work with other persons this pattern often emerges. Even though the fantasy caused her confusion and anguish, it helped point her beyond the helplessness of her marriage to a seeking hope in the future:

My fantasy will continue to enter into my thoughts as long as it continues to accomplish its reason for being here. I do believe God sent it. Then one day, I'll wake up and like an elf it will have accomplished its purpose and once satisfied with it's work will drift away. Right now I can't let it go. I guess it's giving me some sort of hope and comfort in all this torture it's also producing? How contradictory. . . .(8/14/78)

"J" 's struggle with the spiritual task of moving away from nostalgia toward hope persisted over time. She did find some resolution in this task about nine months later:

I saw Jm (fantasized lover). *Went to N* (small town 50 miles away) *1 year after the happening. . . . Yes, I can understand why he sent me last year—it's just a good feeling not to be blown away by him or anyone now! (5/15/79)*

The second cycle of confession, blaming others, and the third cycle, blaming self, often come close together and can be interchangeable. "J" tended to focus responsibility for her discontent on herself, as witnessed by her two years of counseling preceding the initiation of her journal. she began her journal with the emotional expression of depression which is typical of cycle three:

Blue, I'm so tired of being blue. Depression is out to get me. Depression rides with me each day. (8/14/78)

"J" 's thinking in her first journal entry reflects an assumption of blame by questioning her dissatisfaction:

There just must be more to life in the emotional sense of the word than what I've ever had. Is this another "common" problem of women in their 30's. I suppose many people go through life unfulfilled emotionally—I just hate be one of them. Do I expect too much? (8/14/78)

In the case of "J" her expression of anger followed very closely her feelings of guilt but ten days later "J" began to feel mutual responsibility for the marital breakdown and began the emotional bargaining of cycle four.

I believe "THIS MARRIAGE COULD BE SAVED" if Jx (spouse) *could come to me and ask to see T* (clinical psychologist who had been counseling "J") *or suggest anything to save it because he wanted to save it. . . . But where is my fault? Where? It takes 2 people to fuck up a marriage. . . . I do want to work on it, because it is so dangerously close to failure. (8/28/78)*

To this point "J" appears to be moving rapidly through confession, though one will note that so far no mention has been made of the spiritual tasks in cycles two, three or four. In part because "J" had not yet dealt with these spiritual tasks she entered a period of regression.

It's done. I asked him for a divorce and didn't argue. . . . Where did our love go? I can't accept him and he can't accept me. But we're going to T (clinical psychologist) *for one last shot at it. . . .*

> *... it would be easier if we were yelling and screaming and hating.... How can I want to divorce him and not hate him and be angry.... He can't give me what I need emotionally—but am I over looking what he can give me? Am I wanting the moon. My God—the guilt—the desire for something to say that I'm right in this decision.... God! please don't make me wrong in this decision! If we split—let him grow—maybe someway we'll get back together—who knows. (9/1/78)*

Note how "J" pushed right up to the point of asking for the divorce and then backed-off, agreeing to marital counseling "for one last shot at it." Seeking marital counseling is not always a regression. Sometimes the threat of divorce prompts a couple to work seriously at their marriage. The principal reason for this regression was unresolved guilt and anger. Marriage counseling in this case was an attempt to resolve guilt by being sure they had made "every attempt to save the marriage." After two sessions with the clinical psychologist "J" wrote:

> *I want out! I want out! I want out! I could live alone better than like this. My love is gone—I just want T to help both of us exit stage left and right with no guilt to plague us the rest of our lives. (9/18/78)*

Twelve days after the above entry "J" and her husband agreed to divorce and called an attorney to make an appointment. Approximately a month later her husband moved and the divorce papers were signed a few weeks later, but the guilt and shame of cycle three and the anger and resentment of cycle two were still unresolved. Approximately two weeks after the divorce "J" made an appointment with me. During the interview "J" was encouraged to express both her guilt and anger as well as probing in her personal history concerning why she had married Jx. Her journal entry describing this interview illustrates how a pastoral intervention can facilitate movement through the cycle:

> *Had a private conversation with Pastor Bob Hurst (the divorce seminar guide) and he had me crying like a 10 year old. Why'd I marry Jx—money—social status and I thought I loved him. And the reason I couldn't forgive the Rd thing* (another woman spouse had been seeing) *is that I forgave them—him for holding and talking with her—but I couldn't forgive the fact that I wasn't getting held and talked to!! O sweet light of knowledge!! It all falls into place. That guy helped me in 1 hour as much as T did in 2 years!! (11/12/78)*

In this interview "J" made a significant step toward working through the spiritual tasks of cycles two and three. Both anger and guilt persisted in her case. She continued to struggle with the spiritual tasks of "moving from protestations of innocence toward admission of guilt" and "moving from using guilt feelings to evade change of behavior toward attending to the task," even as she tried to work out her dating relationships with other men:

> *I'm not even high and am thinking how paranoid, shaky and otherwise not ready for a special relationship I am.... I cringe to think maybe I was the "skitso" all those years with Jx, doing behaviors I didn't realize were so intolerable to live with. I feel because I can't seem to get emotionally stable, there's some deep seated anger and emotion still left for Jx. (11/29/79)*

A month after the above journal entry "J" finally completed both the spiritual tasks of cycles two and three of confession. While under the influence of drugs on New Years Eve "J" wrote in her journal and finally confronted the deeply repressed truth concerning her ex-spouse's infidelity.

> *One revelation after another when I feel like this. . . . I still want to keep seeing SS* (a new boy friend), *so I will put it off and enjoy his beautiful company—this chance to grow, this chance to kid myself some more about sky blue eyes—like I kidded myself for years about those first sky blue eyes and what did they do, but forsake and ________ Me (why can't I come up with that word—subconsciously I can't accept* yet *that he would do that to* me!*) ME! Pride! that's my hang up! If I have such an over abundance of pride (the Lord wants you humble) then if I had been in the Lord, I would have had the ability and inner strength to accept Jx's* infidelity. *Shame on me. I gotta get into the Lord. (12/31/79)*

Cycle four of confession, "responsibility," has already been mentioned as part of the dynamics which propelled "J" and her ex-spouse into marriage counseling after the decision to divorce had been made. Thoughts of responsibility and emotional expressions of bargaining in this cycle often do not end with the divorce. For instance, three months after the divorce "J" was still dependent on her ex-spouse in some ways:

> *Car stalled, called Jx and he fixed it. . . . Gas is eating me up. Will ask Jx to go halvsies since I'm carting his kids around. (2/4/79)*

Often the spiritual task in cycle four "moving away from nostalgia toward hope" is compelled by outside circumstances. In the case of "J" her ex-spouse's re-marriage occasioned her resolution of this cycle:

> *. . . Jx got married yesterday. How did I feel? A little nostalgic—that's about it. (9/15/79)*

Finishing the past, the fifth cycle of confession, does not come all at once but by degrees. Persons do not need to be finished with denial, blaming or bargaining in order to experience some measure of acceptance. For instance, the first thoughts and emotional expressions of acceptance appear in "J" 's journal entry dated 11/5/78 just a couple of days after Jx moved out:

> *Jx moved out Friday night. It wasn't hard for me like I thought it might be. Packing his stuff wasn't hard either. It's amazing.*
>
> *. . . I've paid the biggest share of my dues and relief is in sight—at least a peace with myself over this thing. That's why I could see my life without Jx so early. (11/5/78)*

"J" 's sense of peace was real in that moment though she would later question whether she had paid the biggest share of her dues. Two other significant entries illustrate "J" 's finishing the past. The first involves the "disposal" of her wedding ring. Pastors need to be aware of how and when a parishioner takes off his/her wedding band. This is a highly symbolic action, and what happens to the ring after it has been removed can be an indication of how the counselee is moving toward accomplishing the spiritual task of accepting the end of the relationship:

> *Ten months I've been on my own. Anxiously awaiting that year anniversary celebration! I was going to exchange my wedding ring for a ring for my birthday—I lost my wedding ring! (8/29/79)*

The second entry which represents a solid sense of finishing was made on the anniversary of the divorce. Just as pastors often contact the bereaved at the anniversary of a death, so also anniversaries of divorces and separations in the parish can be occasions for pastoral concern:

> *So here I am—alone for a year. I have come so far! Biggest accomplishment is the fact that I want to be home with the kids now. . . .*

I am happy to be going to work. I would probably be a working married woman now that the kids are older—the only difference, I wouldn't feel the whole burden myself, if I were married. (11/3/79)

Repentance

Even though "J" increasingly felt finished with the past, she developed a growing sense that she was not finished. Divorce was only part of a solution; she also needed to grow and change. The cycle of repentance begins when the parishioner recognizes the need for personal internal change in addition to the external changes occasioned by the divorce. Even before "J" made her decision to divorce, she was able to begin to express her need for internal change:

. . . but I keep thinking if I can't overcome this in this marriage, I'll just have another big problem in another relationship that might defeat me too. (8/21/78)

While the need for repentance might be glimpsed early in the adjustment process, at least in the case of "J" further repentance work was put off until after the divorce and after she had an opportunity to express more of her guilt and anger. Significantly, in this case the spiritual task of discerning the presence of false consciousness or sin was often linked to her attempts to form new relationships with men. For example this entry which followed her breaking off with her first boy friend after the divorce:

Here I sit with the shakes. . . . I'm fuckin' crazy—not just today—for a long time. Can't stand to be alone. . . .

What would make me feel better? I gotta learn I'm good enough company for me. But I'm so shaky inside—something is stopping me from sitting still. *Can't sit still alone in silence. . . . (12/31/78)*

Unable to sit still alone was a symptom of "J" 's primary problem—in order to feel good about herself she needed the attention of men and as a result she idolized her lovers and made their needs and desires the ultimate value in her life. As time progressed her discernment of this false consciousness grew clearer.

Revelation—Running! Running! . . . I keep thinking some man will come along and fill me up emotionally. . . . But God! I know better! That won't happen. (8/5/79)

I feel so timid, apologetic, subservient, meek, afraid I made SS (boy friend) *mad by something I said. I'm angry at myself. Because I care for him in a big way I'm afraid of losing him, so I'm all these things tonight!—just like with Jx—mousy, insecure—I hate myself! (11/11/79)*

During the two years following the divorce "J" experimented and made many attempts to establish intimate relationships with men. This slow, painful trial and error method finally yielded an insight for "J" concerning her failure in intimate relationships.

I have been screwed figuratively as well as literally. I feel used and stupid. . . . He was just out to have a good time and I was it. . . . He made me feel lowly around him—groveling for attention. Or maybe that's the way I handle intimate relationships. (1/16/80)

Note in the above illustrations the expressions of wonder and determination. Once the veil has parted and the truth is known most counselees want to move ahead. There may be many impasses, even regressions as the individual attempts to move through the rest of the process, but ignorance can no longer be an excuse.

As "J" recognized her own need for change she began to express the hope that she could become different. Entering the second cycle of repentance she began focusing on her negative self-image and dependence by thinking about her ability to be alone:

> *. . . I'm reconstructing my ideas on being alone and having to have someone. I feel in time, I'm going to succeed in learning how to be alone, as I really kinda like to be alone once in a while as opposed to someone who can never bear to be alone. (1/12/79)*

Slowly as "J" reconstructed her thought about aloneness she began to feel encouragement:

> *. . . I'm here alone in the house now—I love it. I think lots better alone, I'm pretty up, though not ecstatic—more cautious—age maybe. (4/4/79)*

The spiritual task of cycle two of repentance requires the counselee to use his/her determination and encouragement to work at identifying specific behaviors resulting from false consciousness and imaging change. In her journal "J" specified four areas in which she began to image transformation. The first entry which indicates advancement to the spiritual task in cycle two focuses on the need for friendship in intimate relationships. Note this entry occurred about 10 months after the divorce, about the same time she was also earnestly working on the spiritual task of the fifth cycle of confession: accepting the end of the relationship.

> *Basically, I'm becoming more stable . . . I'm kinda disinterested in guys . . . have realized if I don't have feelings for a guy, knowing him a little, I'm not up for it. Sex for sex's sake like in the beginning isn't for me. (8/29/79)*

With the passage of time "J" made further progress. A month and a half after the previous entry and preparing to end the relationship already mentioned, "J" identified her own need for assertiveness. if she was to develop a more positive self-image.

> *I find with SS* (boy friend) *as with Jx* (ex-spouse), *I don't stand up for myself as well as I might if I weren't so fuckin' scared of losing him.* That's *bullshit. That's the biggest crap I pulled in my marriage—no balls. And I'm doing exactly that with SS. Somedays I stand up better than others. (1/7/80)*

Finally "J" specifically identified her need to communicate honestly, if friendship was to have a chance:

> *With SC* (a new boy friend) *I'm making no bones about where I'm coming from—* Friendship—*I'm going to be open and verbal so he gets no misconceptions about my intentions. (2/6/80)*

As "J" 's identification of false consciousness and her imaging of change became increasingly specific, she began to express the realization that not only could she be different, the future could be different. Because she could change in the present, the future would be different. Earlier in the process, when a parishioner attempts to move away from nostalgia and look for hope in the future, the future does not hold the same assurance which emerges in cycle three of repentance, when behavior change is initiated:

> *. . . I'm being myself and if he doesn't want me as myself, someday maybe I'll find someone who does. I am so happy with this feeling. The weekend at the church* (previously described) *fixed this in my mid. I worked long and hard to achieve this goal. I arrived and my life is good. (3/14/80)*

Knowing the future could be different gave "J" the confidence to contemplate alternative futures. She found the more she worried about remarriage the worse her dating relationships worked out. Note the confidence and hopefulness in the following entry:

> *I find often the thought, "Hey, there might just be another successful way to live besides being married." I don't feel so frantic to get married. I'll do the next relationship different—commitment— being true to myself . . . (5/21/80)*

The spiritual task of cycle three in repentance might be described as specific appropriate penance—or changing self by changing behavior. Up to this point the spiritual tasks of repentance have primarily been accomplished through revelation and discernment—gifts of grace. In cycle three, grace is primarily mediated through works. This is the hard effort of practicing virtue until it becomes integrated into the personality.

> *By myself today. Doing good things—really—laundry, grocery shopping, jogging—2 miles!! With Lent I'm fasting on Wednesday, exercising each day, praying each day and giving up R's* (a local tavern).[7] *Making myself stronger. I need a good reason to give up R's. . . . (3/11/79)*

The pastor can be influential and helpful in assisting the parishioner to make creative behavior changes. Note the use of Lenten disciplines of denial in the entry above. The penitential traditions of Lent can transform painful necessities into virtues. Also pastors can pay attention to the relationship between physical and spiritual exercise.

As "J" 's identification of her problem became more clearly defined in cycle two of repentance, her behavior changes became more specific in cycle three:

> *. . . I called him and he said he had changed his mind and that he wasn't coming. I was so disappointed, hurt and mad, and now thankful. He is selfish and slick tongued. . . . I'm mad because he has the power to crunch me so. Fucking Shit of being involved with someone. You are laid open to them . . . at least I told him I was disappointed—I'm going to teach myself to stand up more and more. (1/13/80)*

In the above entry "J" notes her own change of behavior "at least I told him I was disappointed." Her "thankfulness" expressed in the entry can be interpreted as a recognition of personality change resulting from this behavior change. "J" even became aggressive later in her willingness to communicate her feelings:

> *I told him I was going to start speaking up when I didn't like how things are going—going to nail him to the cross! He said that was fine as long as I didn't hit him. (1/24/80)*

One of the most decisive behavior changes occurred when "J" decided not to have sex with a new boy friend because of her discovery that her physical intimacy without emotional and spiritual commitment ruined the growth and development of emotional and spiritual intimacy:

> *The peace I got together at the awareness weekend* (already described above) *was almost tangible—all pervasive of my person. Upon making love to SC* (boy friend), *when you'd think I'd be happy and content, doubts and fears were all around me. When I let him go—decided that making love without marriage was totally against my being—the Peace returned. (5/8/80)*

In the realization of changing self by changing behavior in the entry above there appears the emotional expression of peace. "J" finally had a normative experience to judge her spiritual health. Whenever she regressed, she could sense her misdirection in her prayer life.

FORGIVENESS

One and a half years after the divorce "J" was finally able to express the sense of forgiveness which comes from becoming a new person. This forgiveness is deeper than the earlier feeling of being finished with the past. This is a forgiveness which reaches into the future as one is graced to become a new person in Christ.

All my problems are the same as yesterday. But because I've got this Peace, I've got no doubts or fears. He's (God) *got them. I'll never let another man take this Peace from me! (5/8/80)*

Same problems as I had while I was so discontent, but now I'm so full of peace and the ability to handle these same problems—amazing! I'm doing something right. (5/21/80)

Even though "J" experienced several regressions in the months following these entries, she had developed the inner mechanisms of self-direction which enabled her largely on her own to work through her impasses and to continue moving through the process:

Spiritually I'm growing so fast! My quiet time in the morning is a must *now. I'm working on patience with the kids. . . . I pray when I'm dealing with the kids—it's working. I'm reading* God Calling—*this is the best time of all. . . . The Lord took SC* (most recent boy friend) *from me, because I was idolizing him as I did Jx* (ex-spouse). *By taking him away the Lord is #1 and when I've concretized that, lived with it for a while, maybe he'll send me someone. (6/9/80)*

In the above entry seeds of the second cycle of forgiveness, and the finishing of the adjustment process, can be discerned. "J" is expressing a new growing intimacy with her children, with God, and even sees the possibility of a special relationship with someone of the opposite sex in the future. "J" also finds to her surprise she is expressing love in giving to someone else—her children—rather than frantically trying to get love sexually from a man. Finally, "J" has expressed an openness to the future which is faith.

SUMMARY

This paper has presented a model of divorce adjustment in terms of spiritual direction to provide pastors with a theological understanding of the process. An underlying assumption has been that ministry to the divorced can grow out of professional models grounded in the practice of ministry,

Six important understandings emerge from the case study of "J" and the presentation of divorce adjustment in terms of spiritual direction.

First, the model of divorce adjustment presented in this paper is grounded in the tradition of the church. Confession, repentance, forgiveness are concepts deeply rooted in the history of the care of souls. Pastors utilizing this model can feel they are practicing their pastoral expertise.

Second, the key to understanding movement in this model is found in the accomplishment of spiritual tasks. Parishioners can be encouraged to experience their therapeutic work as part of their over all spiritual development. Again the process is grounded in a genuine area of pastoral competence—spiritual direction.

Third, the model presented in this paper is future oriented. "Finishing the past" is not enough. What the person is becoming is as important in this model as where he/she has been. New intimacy, if not defined exclusively in terms of remarriage or sexual relationships, is an appropriate goal in the Christian life.

Fourth, the model presented fits the schedule of the pastor. Parishioners, like "J", can be encouraged to take initiative in making contact when they need help. There were some significant pastoral interventions in "J" 's case, but there was by no means regular weekly contact. This model encourages the possibility of "checking in" from time to time, rather than weekly visits. So long as the counselee is moving intervention is not necessary. Whenever a parishioner is "stuck" the model can help the pastor discern the unfinished task, and help the person to get moving again. This rhythm of contact more nearly fits the schedule of the pastor than the weekly therapeutic hour.

Fifth, the case study of "J" helps to illustrate the larger context of the church community in pastoral care. At the time of her divorce "J" was a lapsed member of a fundamentalist church, which condemned divorce. "J" was most interested in the divorce adjustment seminar led by my wife and me, because it was offered in a church setting. After the ten week seminar she began involving herself in some church activities. By the time of the last cited entry in her journal, June of 1980, she had become a regular worship attendant and was facilitated in her movement by her participation in the larger life of the parish.

Sixth, the case study of "J" offers an excellent illustration of the therapeutic value of journal keeping. Especially in the New Year's Eve 1979 entry the writing down of her feelings provided an opportunity for expression under unusual circumstances, which might never have been available in a counseling session. The keeping of a journal can be an important part of spiritual direction in the divorce adjustment process.

While the model presented in this paper might be helpful to other professionals practicing in the field of divorce adjustment counseling, pastors are most uniquely prepared to offer the "ritual" interventions and spiritual interpretations suggested by this conceptual approach. Certainly "J" 's story demonstrates how deepened spiritual life can grow out of the struggle to adjust to divorce. The case study also holds open the possibility that adjustment to a divorce can be facilitated by growth in the spiritual life of the individual. Pastors can be encouraged to think of themselves as significant and uniquely helpful resource for the divorced.

1. One significant exception is Dr. Joseph Federico, Director of the Divorce Adjustment Institute of Evanston, Illinois. His work in "marital separation and re-direction" has emphasized the "obsessive review" of the divorced as an opportunity for change and growth.
2. Kenneth Kressel, "Patterns of Coping in Divorce and Some Implications for Clinical Practice," *Family Relations* 29 (April 1980) p. 236.
3. A note concerning this case study is appropriate. When I was trying to decide how to illustrate a theory which had been developed over the course of four years and many counseling contacts, my advisor,Dr. Philip Anderson,suggested the use of a case study. As I considered the many persons with whom I had worked, one woman stood out in my mind as having been typical and exemplary. We had worked together off and on over a two year period. When I approached her to ask her permission and cooperation to use her as a case study, she most graciously said, "yes." Then she asked me, "I have been keeping a journal for the last two years, would that be of any help to you?"

   Without my knowlege she had been keeping a journal. When I began examining her journal entries,I recognized that this offered an unusual opportunity for case study material. Here were the thoughts and feelings of a counselee expressed in a private journal, without the need to rely upon the memory, the notes and possible misinterpretations of a counselor. I would like to acknowledge my deep appreciation of "J" for offering her journal for use, and trust that the reader will also recognize the unusual opportunity for understanding which this material affords.

4. Robert Moore, "Dynamics of the Demonic in Movement Terms," a chart offered in the course "Minister as Spiritual Director," Spring 1980, the Chicago Theological Seminary.
5. Joseph Federico, interview held at the Divorce Adjustment Institute, Evanston, Illinois, November 1977.
6. In the state where this divorce occurred, there is no legal waiting period. In the particular county where the legal papers were filed, the Judiciary and the Bar expedite divorce cases. Most cases require little more than a week from the time one party contacts an attorney to final court action.
7. The "good things" mentioned in this entry were suggested to "J" in a counseling session at the beginning of Lent 1979. The daily prayer time and fasting on Wednesdays had been recommended in the church newsletter. Pastors can make use of the larger life of the parish, even the newsletter, in their counseling.
8. The following entry from "J's" journal demonstrates how the Sunday morning sermon can become part of the larger context of pastoral care in the parish setting:

His sermon yesterday hit home—be receptive to God's blessings. I feel like I am—don't do anything you consciously know is wrong and spend an hour a day by myself and I'll do alright. . . . it's so reassuring to hear this—we all need reassuring. (6/2/80)

CHAPTER III

A Response To Pastor-Client Sexual Relations

by Ann Bartram

On a humid July day I was feeling hot, sticky and irritable as I saw clients on the hour. Why aren't ministers' offices air-conditioned? Coupled with these complaints were my own personal problems which had me feeling raw and fragile at that moment. Jayne, my three o'clock appointment, had just left, and I opened the door to greet Tom, my last client for the day.

There he stood, one of my favourite and most interesting clients, looking the elegant jock he is, even in the July heat. White suit, pin stripe cream and brown shirt with coordinated brown silk tie, fresh from his air-conditioned car and his air-conditioned Bay Street office, he looked on top of life.

I caught his eyes and felt him take me in and as he did I saw his expression of concern. I leaned into the non-verbal communication and felt the vibrant electricity that is so indescribable but unmistakable—the chemistry of sexual attraction flaring between us. I suppose I hoped what I was feeling hadn't happened, and I let it pass. Tom sat down and made to let it pass also. He began to talk very fast, straight out of his head, avoiding any eye contact with me.

What would I do? Would I call him on his behaviour or ignore it? It had been in the air before this occurrence. It is my style as a counsellor to call a person to what they are feeling. These thoughts flashed quickly through my head and I made my decision.

"Tom, stop! What were you feeling just a moment ago when you came into my office?"

Tom stopped and grew very still. His eyes caught mine and flew away. Again the chemistry between us filled the room. "No way, Ann, I'm not going to tell you. Look, it makes my hands tremble to even consider it."

"Tom, I think that you had better say what you are feeling now. It is what there is." I speak softly, and I feel a mixture of excitement and fear.

"Look, Ann, when I came in the door, you looked down, sort of hurting. (pause) I've never seen you like this before. (longer pause) I am really attracted to you, and I just want to hold you." Tom looked embarrassed and uncertain.

Inside me flashed the recognition of just how much I'd like to be held.

This is a vignette from my personal case load as a specialist in pastoral counselling. It is presented as a graphic illustration of the presence of sexual feelings in a counselling hour.

Elsie came to me for help when she discovered that her pastor, who was counselling her, was having sexual relations not only with her but also with her friend and fellow parishioner.

Jenny was referred to me by the third male pastor from whom she had sought help. With the first two she had had intimate sexual relations.

A pastor came to me stricken with guilt because he was having sexual relations with a very fragile and hurting woman in his parish.

Such experiences as a pastoral counsellor lead me to the seriousness of the question: "How will I respond to sexual feelings in myself, in my parishioner, in both of us, when and if they arise?" More questions follow in rapid succession as I attempt to answer this one question. Will I suppress, ignore, deny, avoid and/or sublimate these feelings? Will I act or not act on them, and what will guide that decision? Will I allow them to be aired and explored as I would any other feeling arising in the counselling context?

An obvious, time honoured and respectable solution to what to do in the presence of sexual feelings and their urgency is to obey a rule. This rule might be expressed as, a pastor must not act out sexually with a client. Professional organizations in the field of mental health have had such a rule at the heart of their ethical codes from the beginning.

I have two problems with this, one pragmatic and one theological. First, the rule has not been totally effective. The statistical data indicates that this is an important ethical and therapeutic struggle not only for the pastor but also for all professionals working in the field. Masters and Johnson conclude, as a result of listening to their female patients who claimed that they had sexual relations with a previous therapist, that, if only twenty five percent of these reports of seductions are true, then it is a very prevalent phenomenon.[1] When in 1976 Masters and Johnson drew together a conference to discuss the ethical concerns of sex therapy, the liveliest topic drawing the most participation was the subject of patient-therapist sex.

The church and the profession of pastoral counsellors have not tackled this controversial problem with much openness. Charles Rassieur, Director of the Institute of Pastoral Counseling in Harrisburg, Pennsylvania, courageously researched the topic and in 1976 produced a book, *The Problem Clergymen Don't Talk About.* He makes very clear that it is indeed a problem that ordinary and very fine pastors face often in the pastorate.

It is interesting to note that the topic of sexual relations between a pastor and parishioner seeking help is not a new phenomenon only seen in the post sexual revolution seventies and eighties.[2] Rather, it has a long history in the church.

Boccaccio's *Decameron,* written in the 1300's and one of the earliest printed books (1471), testifies to similar activity between monk and a lay woman of his parish. The fourth novel of the first day tells, with gentle humour, how a young monk and his superior, the abbot, both have intercourse with a young woman of the district on the same day.

> He (the abbot) drew near the girl, and softly bade her be comforted, and besought her not to weep; and so little by little he came at last to show her where he would be at . . . he refrained from lying upon her but laid her upon him, and in that manner deported himself with her for a long time.[3]

Secondly, and from the theological perspective, rules speak of legalism to me. Paying due respect to this and at the same time paying attention to the ethic of love given by Jesus compels me to open myself to the whole question of pastor/client sexual feelings in a dialogical way open to grace and compassion.

Thus this paper is written to confront and open for discussion the issue of how to respond in the presence of pastor/client sexual feelings in the counselling context. It is written from a female perspective and the uniqueness and strength of this is offered without apology. I shall share four concerns that have guided my decision and response to this increasingly important issue. Then I shall offer my own therapeutic approach to the presence of sexual feelings in the counselling relationship by returning to the continued verbatim of the hour between Tom and myself.

In my research I endeavoured to open myself as thoroughly as possible to the position most clearly articulated by John Money, a professor in the John Hopkins School of Medicine. He comments, "I'm trying to take a glimpse into history, twenty five years from now, and I suspect we might find that we're extraordinarily old-fashioned in our ideas on sexual intercourse in relation to therapy."[4]

I am not in my heart a conservative person. Yet after a long ethical struggle much guided by James Nelson's work in his book *Embodiment,* I find that I could not support engagement in pastor-client sexual relations at this moment in history. Yet I cautiously allow that this is not a fixed and closed position but open to dialogue with my peers and open to unique circumstances.

What do I mean by pastor-client sexual relations? This is an important question as many of us as counsellors employ a form of therapy that involves a great deal of body touching. In referring to pastor-client sexual relations, I mean any overt sexual play in the presence of sexual feeling from hand holding to oral sex, from foot massage to genital intercourse, from sexual touching to verbal seduction.

Four concerns have led me to the position of not acting out upon sexual feelings as they occur in the context of counselling. The first of these comes as a response to the question, Who am I in this moment of time? Let me answer the question by sharing who I am on that July day when Tom came into my office.

I am hot, sticky and irritable. I am not at my best. I wish the day were over, that my holidays yet three weeks away had already begun and that I could go swimming. I am angry that my needs for pleasure are blocked.

As well I have several personal problems that press for attention. My husband and I are teetering on the edge of estrangement in mid-life crisis time. Our son has written from camp to say that he hates it for the first time in years and would we come and fetch him home. He is in the throes of adolescent love and missing the girl down the street. My mother writes of the overwhelming loneliness and pain she endures this first summer since Dad died. I am a burdened person.

Years of experience have taught me that this is often the way it is for a pastor. We are very human and often are pastors because we are searchers with many of life's questions unanswered in our souls. I believe that this is very normal. There are, of course, periods of remarkable clarity and strength, but there are always times when we are exceedingly hurting and vulnerable.

Butler and Zelen's study of twenty counsellors who had sexual relations with their clients, while admittedly a small sample, indicated that, "Ninety percent reported having been 'vulnerable,' 'needy,' and/or 'lonely' when the sexual contact occurred."[5]

It is my concern at this point that to act sexually with a client so easily could have more to do with my needs than theirs. It is not that my need is necessarily inappropriate but that to act on it with a client is both inappropriate and therapeutically destructive in the sense that it would rob the therapeutic moment of its deeper potential for growth.

Also, part of knowing who I am involves knowing what kind of person most likely attracts me. Often counselors are very clear about this; for example, a man may know that five foot six inch, shapely brunette women who are ten years younger attract him. Other counsellors are less precise, but it is important to consider the question.

Tom is for me an attractive man. I will share why as I feel that men and women may differ here as to what is attractive to them. Tom is an executive in a tough competitive field, and he is successful. He likes his work and is a powerful presence. One day in my office he broke down and wept. I began to be attracted as his softer side emerged.

I note with interest that when the sexual feelings surfaced between us to the point of verbalization, they did so with Tom assuming the role of aggressor. "I just want to hold you," rather than "I want to be held." The traditionally enculturated woman in me lurks always under the surface to find an aggressive male pleasing.

I also found Tom strikingly physically fit and attractive, four years younger than myself. He shared his sexual fantasies with me from time to time, and they were lively and imaginative. Having to talk with him about sexual matters heightened the chemistry between us.

I have stated this so audaciously and explicitly because I suspect that what I find attractive in a male differs from a male counsellor's affectional orientation. For me, a friendly, outgoing, physically fit and successful man who is actively pursuing emotional growth and maturity can prompt sexual feelings in me regardless of age, physical beauty, handicaps and race. Who I am means knowing this about myself.

It is a general opinion that if the pastor's sexual relation with his or her spouse is warm and fulfilling, that pastor then will be less likely to be attracted to the client. Charles Rassieur challenges this opinion directly:

> It must be understood that this process of sexual attraction is basically unrelated to the degree of sexual satisfaction a pastor feels about his own marriage.[6]

While I disagree with 'basically unrelated,' I do believe that Rassieur sounds a valid cautionary note.

The early 1960's film *Le Bonheur* caught this dilemma so poignantly in the days before the emergence of open marriage. In the film the husband loves the wife fully and beautifully. In the rush of these good feelings he loves a second woman with similar passion. For him, it is as simple as the analogy, if one apple in the orchard is very good there is every expectation that the next apple will be delicious also. It is dangerous to assume that because the primary relationship is adequate that as a pastor you will not be attracted to a client.

The complexity of the task of knowing who I am leads me to conclude that to act sexually with a client would be fraught with my own unresolved needs.

My second concern in choosing not to act sexually with a client has evolved over years of practice. It has to do with the nature of the pastor-client covenant or contract.

My understanding of this bond has developed over time. Early in my counselling career I thought of counselling as something that had a beginning, a journey and an end. That is how it was for me initially; but then I found that, in response to crisis or an increased need to know myself more fully, I wanted to do more of my own therapy. I began to accept that my therapeutic journey did not have a clear end but only welcome interruptions. I discovered that my experience in this regard was paralleled by the experience of my clients.

Thus led by my experience and that of my clients I came to a new and fuller understanding of the pastor-client bond or covenant. I have come to see myself as a counsellor who, in taking on a client, takes on that person for life. I will be available to that person over time when and if that person seeks my help. I am more and more of a life consultant.

This is also a pastoral issue. Being ministered unto is not a once-in-a-life-time experience. The words of the resurrected Christ model for the pastor a fresh challenge: "And be assured, I am with you always, to the end of time." (Matt. 28:20) As the pastor-counsellor responds to this challenge, the bond grows in richness and begins to include participation with the client in celebrating the joyous moments as well as the painful ones. Such a pastor may find herself being asked to marry, to participate in baptism and to rejoice with a client. Increasingly this raises the important question of the specialist in pastoral counseling being closely related to the life of a church community in a recognized manner.

Out of such a covenant or contract, what does it mean if I have a sexual relationship with Tom? It feels to me that it would deeply muddy and unnecessarily complicate our contract, my part of which is that I will be for him over time. In fact it may well violate that important covenant totally.

In reflecting on my case load, I came to see that it was precisely at the point of understanding the nature of the counsellor-client contract in the context of sexual feelings that problems escalated in the therapeutic relationships sustained by Elsie and Jenny. Both women wanted and sought an enduring and sustaining relationship with their pastors. They felt, when they shared their bodies with their pastor and he responded in kind, that a new covenant was being forged, the nature of which was in process. The women clearly hoped and felt that they were moving out of the pastor-parishioner mode of relating toward a love relationship between equals that would one day involve full commitment and possibly marriage. They fantasized often that they were the lady of the manse.

John Money supports this experience of Elsie and Jenny:

> It seems to me in all the cases I've known in which the therapist has broken the initial contract which was to talk with the patient, and begun a communication of body language in sexual contact or sexual intercourse itself, the problem has been that patient wanted to fall in love with the therapist and not just have sex.[7]

I sense an important distinction here between men and women at this point in history. Women still connect sexual intercourse, love and commitment very powerfully together. (Traditional women make this connection but also, perhaps strangely, so do many women of a strong feminist persuasion who see themselves as sexually liberated. Germane Greer's new book, *Sex and Destiny* is particulaly revealing and challenging on just this point.) It seems to me that, as women, we make this link to create a climate of trust and security. This, then, allows the full expression of sexuality to blossom as it can only when controls are surrendered. I often feel that men do not so deeply bond full sexual expression with surrender of control.

Is there really a male/female difference in this area? Is such a difference, if it exists, biological or enculturated? I do not have final answers but I suggest that the questions are very important and their existence ought to inform a pastor when he or she makes a decision to be or not to be sexually intimate with a parishioner.

As a pastor I intend to offer myself as a counsellor to a client for life. This for me is a valuable, worthy, therapeutic, and Christian covenant. Present experience of men and women indicates that the expression of sexual relations between a pastor and a parishioner in need significantly changes—perhaps, more for women than men—the nature of that covenant and ultimately may violate it completely.

Closely related to this issue is my third concern—the unequal nature for the contractual relationship between counselor and client, pastor and her parishioner. I agree with Susan Brownmiller when she says, "The imposition of sex by an authority figure is hardly consensual or equal."[8] The parishioner who seeks the help of the pastor in a time of crisis sees that pastor as an authority figure, Christ's representative on earth. This is also true of the parishioner who comes in order to grow and mature. A competent pastor acknowledges and accepts this power and uses it to promote healing. A pastor-client relationship is a one up, one down relationship that may over time move towards moments of genuine peer sharing. The nature of the pastor-client contract exludes equal assent to sexual relationship.

For this reason Susan Brownmiller, William Masters, Phyllis Chesler, and others have been led to the radical stance that therapist-client sex is nothing less than rape. In the pastoral context I find this judgment harsh; the data of my cases, wherein a pastor and client acted sexually indicates that there was a deepening though troubled commitment toward loving each other. Still, in my opinion, meaningful and nonexploitative sexual activity is something engaged in between equals and, at the point of sexual action, the pastor and the client radically change the counselling contract.

The unequal nature of the counselling contract has to be seen from a feminist perspective as well. Women have a long history of abuse as the underdog in sexual relations. The statistical data on the incidence of therapist-client sexual relations shows clearly that the woman is most often the patient. A leading American sex therapist, Helen Kaplan, confirms this when she states:

> *There is a relatively high incidence of male therapists having sexual experiences with female patients, in contrast with rather rare instances when female therapists are attracted to and have sex with male patients.*[9]

Continuing in this vein, I feel it necessary to note that traditionally women have submitted to authority figures whereas men have been encouraged either to hold their own or rebel in the face of authority. Consequently a female client will be more apt to submit to the sexual desires of her pastor and a female pastor less likely to initiate sexual activity with a male client.

Even as these cultural attitudes change due to the feminist movement and the male finds himself actively sexually pursued by his more liberated female client, there is the possibility that new neurotic patterns are emerging. The female client's response may be based in the hostility of the oppressed.

Let me not leave this concern without acknowledging that it is possible to dissolve a contract or convenant and forge a new one. Pastors and clients have made new covenants of friendship that may or may not include sexual expression and may or may not include living together or marriage. Freud encouraged one of his analysts to marry a client. William Reich did and there are a growing number of permanent relationships that have issued from what as first a counseling relationship.

My note of caution here would be that the dissolving of a covenant or contract is serious business and must be felt and grieved over time before any new healthy contract can emerge. There are those who claim that the pastor/client covenant is as indissolvable as that between a parent and child. While I do not agree with this position, it does signal for me the gravity of the action. It also intrigues me to think not only of the dissolution of a covenant but also of the transformation of a covenant in this instance.

My fourth and last concern that informs my decision not to act sexually with a client is rooted in the difficult understanding of what constitutes healing. A psychotherapeutic principle for me as a counsellor is, I am not there for my client in order to 'do' something. Engaging in sexual relations with a client certainly can be viewed as doing something for or with the client. It runs the danger of making the pastor into a rescuer and the client into victim or persecutor, thus successfully blocking real growth.

Theologically I understand this principle in the context of reinforcing God's passionate commitment to each person. God offers to us infinite trust that we are creative and able to make unique responses and discover our own direction. This is made abundantly vivid for us in God's affirmation of David. David and his men are making a getaway from Saul, and they are hungry. They arrive at the shrine at Nob and Ahimelech. The priest assures them the available bread is consecrated and that it is only for the ritually pure to eat. David and his men need that bread, and David maneuvers the situation so that he and his men eat the bread. He reinterprets what is meant by holy so that it is holy that David become king. David acts in new ways, and the energy for such action is rooted in David's assurance that God believed in him.

As counselling pastors we are called to believe in God's commitment to each person, each client we see. Within that person and within ourselves lies the potential for newness, new acts, new ways of being. Our job as pastors is to trust that commitment, to trust the creativity that lies within and to call it forth rather than to 'do' for another.

How can I as counselling pastor be part of the healing process with my hurting parishioner? If 'doing' something for my client does not heal, what *does* constitute healing? This is an enormous question yielding in this century the emergence of a great variety of schools of therapy, each with its own variations of what is healing.

As I understand the nature of my practice and at the risk of over simplication, I see people who are for the most part intellectually competent and emotionally undernourished. I see people who think logically and beautifully and who feel only the barest minimum. The balance is awry. The degree of imbalance varies a great deal and is possibly greater in males than in females in the western world at this time. Healing occurs when the client begins to feel more deeply and regains a balance in feeling and thinking out of which healthier decisions, engraved though they may be with ambiguity, begin to flow.

Given these observations, I also see the root problem for most of my clients and or myself as a lack of self esteem, a deep seated lack of self worth. Theologically we fail to accept God's passionate commitment to us that would free our creative resources. Healing comes when this belief is reborn, belief in our essential goodness in spite of our brokenness. Many blocked feelings and thoughts stand in the way of this belief and trouble it and diminish it. Recovery lies in feeling what is blocked with the skilled help of the pastor counsellor.

In keeping with this theoretical orientation I encourage my client to feel whatever emerges for them without sanction or judgment. All feelings are acceptable, from murderous rage through sexual aggresssion to an outpouring of altruistic love. To feel a feeling and discover its origin within is one thing but to act on that feeling is quite another. Don Browning, professor of pastoral care at the University of Chicago, gives us a helpful word about accepting feelings:

> Pastoral counselling to some extent brackets moral issues and focuses more specifically on emotional dynamic issues that block persons from living the kind of life they hope for and believe in.[10]

Thus we are given the idea of bracketing moral issues for a time and, as a client explores her feelings, the pastor allows and accepts, aware of the bracketing. As I have practiced, over and over I find that after allowing feelings to emerge, no matter how immoral, in time the client herself returns to the moral implications and spontaneously makes extremely moral decisions.

What constitutes healing in my therapeutic method is a firm commitment to the client's inalienable right to feel and be whatever and whoever she is at any given moment of time. Prior to acting on that feeling she needs to explore the feeling in all the ways she can with the help of the pastor until she knows both emotionally and rationally what it means for her life. Only then will the appropriate action emerge. Thus to act on sexual feelings with a client would be to rob both the pastor and the client of all the potential for growth inherent in the desire.

These four concerns (who I am in my vulnerability, concern for the nature of the covenant made with a client, recognizing and accepting that counselling is a relationship between unequals and a concern for what consititutes healing) have led me to make the decision not to act on sexual feelings that emerge in the context of counselling. However, I am still left with the question, how will I respond when sexual feeling emerges in the context of counselling?

The opening illustration of the dialogue between Tom and me makes very clear that sexual feelings can and will emerge from time to time in any pastor's experience. They often arise in a mild stirring of chemistry or they may emerge in the form of an erection or definite vaginal lubrication. As early as June, 1960, Nathaniel Lehrman reminds us:

> Whenever two people work very closely together toward a common goal with at least fair success, as a minister does with his parishioner, or a doctor with his patient, feelings of camaraderie and warmth almost inevitably arise between them. When the two people are of the opposite sex, and not too disparate in background, these warm feelings will almost always assume a sexual cast.[11]

It is normal and to be expected that, from time to time, sexual feelings will occur within the counselling experience.

Carl Rogers states, "In many current psychotherapies the very process of psychotherapy engenders sharing and intimacy."[12]

This may be particularly true of the body therapies such as bioenergetics where physical touch is a prescribed part of the healing process. The body of the therapist and client are in frequent contact, often in a structured manner but also spontaneously. Since touching in our society is often a powerful trigger to sexual feeling and arousal, therapists who work with the body must be acutely aware of the the possible emergence of a strong sexual response either in themselves and/or in their clients. Increasingly as pastors use these techniques of touching in their counselling, they too will find themselves more frequently in the presence of sexual feeling.

How can counselling proceed when the commitment is not to act on these sexual feelings by becoming sexually involved with the client? Counsellors have a variety of paths. Some refuse to talk about sexual feelings in the pastor-client relationship, knowing full well that such talk can escalate the feeling. Others focus on and talk of their own happy marriages or love life. These paths do not explore the full potential for growth that such feelings release.

In keeping with my fourth concern (that what constitutes healing is, in the first instance, feeling deeply whatever emerges) it is my contention that, in the presence of sexual feeling, the client needs to be encouraged to centre on that feeling. If the pastor has the feeling, she needs to engage in some therapeutic work exploring that feeling for herself.

When a client is feeling anger within the therapeutic relationship, for example toward the pastor, the feeling can be encouraged and expressed verbally or non verbally by hitting something soft and appropriate. Likewise feelings of joy, pain and fear can be expressed and followed until their meaning becomes clear both emotionally and intellectually. These feelings may be clear and healthy responses on which decisions can be made, or they may be muddied by complex neurotic patterns yeilding decisions which entrap the client in familiar ways. The pastor helps the client in this journey of checking out the purity of the feeling she has.

What follows is a verbatim into which I have inserted reflections. It is indeed flawed and this reflects the high anxiety that accompanies the presence of real sexual feelings in the counselling context. Nevertheless it is an attempt to allow and stay with the feeling in the room rather than block it. At the time of this counselling episode, I had seen Tom and his wife Ali for forty sessions of one hour each. When they first came to see me, their marriage was severely dislocated due to Tom's having a vasectomy in a burst of anger without consulting with his wife who in fact wanted the option of having children. The crisis over forty sessions was resolved in a creative way for them both. Ali then contracted to see me individually, sporadically as she desired. Conjoint sessions were to be held every six to eight weeks or as desired, and Tom contracted to continue working primarily on his own growth as a response to some of his learnings from the conjoint sessions. This is a verbatim from very early in the individual sessions.

Ann: Tom, stop! What were you feeling just a moment ago when you came into my office?

At this point, very early in the hour I have made the decision to follow my hunch that there are sexual feelings in the air. It is not the first time I have worked with them in my own therapy and feel ready to encourage Tom, if in fact my hunch is accurate.

Tom: No way, Ann, I'm not going to tell you. Look, it makes my hands tremble.

Ann: Tom, I think you had better share what you're feeling right now. It is what you are in touch with.

Tom: Look, Ann, when I came in the door, you looked very down to-day, sort of hurting. (pause) I've never seen you like that. (longer pause) I am really attracted to you and I just want to hold you.

Ann: There is a large part of me that would like to be held by you.

Tom: But I couldn't do that, Ann . . . like you're . . . I'm not together enough to hold someone like you. Christ, Ann, what does this mean? I'm attracted you. I guess I've always wanted to be dominated by a woman.

Ann: At least it is out in the open now. You feel attracted to me. I want you to know . . .

Helen Kaplan states, "In actual practice (referring to sex therapy) however, erotic transferences seldom occur if the therapist is not overtly or covertly seductive."[13]

Tom has said that he is attracted to me and that he has always wanted to be dominated by a woman. I completely ignore this powerful statement and go back to his attraction for me. Here I am clearly and unwisely seductive, and I miss a great therapeutic opportunity. Such flaws are, in my experience, later recoverable, which is comforting but not excusing. Later Tom and I were to focus on the issue of domination by a woman at a very deep level finding rage at this mother and a decision to hurt women as a way of getting his mother back.

Tom: Yeh, you want me to know that it's normal. I felt attracted to Ed (his former therapist who referred Tom and his wife to me) and wanted to see more of him but the way I feel about you is very different.

Ann: Tom, it is normal but that's not what I was going to say. (laughing) It's that the attraction is going both ways. I feel it as well. That makes it more complicated.

To share or not share my own sexual feelings is a controversial question. Conventional wisdom would recommend that I do not. Yet I have chosen to, and I do so, for it is important to me to be as honest as I can be unless there is a therapeutic reason to withold information as, for example, in going after a projection. I am having sexual feelings, and they are going to make doing therapy a more treacherous journey. I think Tom has a right to know that. I feel it is an opportunity to let my humanness show. It has the potential power to allow Tom's creativeness more room. To keep hidden the fact that I have sexual feelings also makes me unnecessarily one up in the session.

Is this care? Perhaps it is more than Tom can handle. It comes to me that it would be best to check out with Tom, "Would you like to know how I feel?" or to wait for Tom to enquire.

Tom: So what do we do—stop therapy and go to bed? I go to another therapist? Maybe we should go back to joint sessions with Ali. Geeus—what does this mean about what I feel for Ali? I want to go to bed with you.

Ann: Ali and you have never talked about what you will do if either of you gets turned on elsewhere?

Tom: No way! Ali . . . I don't think she'd like to hear that.

Ann: You never walk down the street and say to her, "Hey, there's a cute chick (their word)—she appeals to me?"

Tom: No, never.

Ann: Do you ever feel that?

Tom: All the time!

At this point the issue of Tom and my feelings finds its place in a larger context. It is evident by his vocal expression that Tom enjoys feeling attracted to women. He has not resolved this with Ali, his wife. It would have been important to follow this theme. It may be a perfectly healthy response, or it may be that Tom sexualizes much of his life and is trapped by this.

Tom's response is an important clue here to the process of therapy. Suppose he had answered, "Never!" or "I've never felt sexual before to-day." Therapy would then proceed by staying with how that felt, to feel sexual for the first time. It might feel frightening and it might feel joyful, and therapy would have to respond appropriately.

Ann: I suspect that Ali feels the same way about other men from time to time.

Tom: Yeh, but it is not part of our contract in marriage to talk about how we feel about members of the opposite sex. In fact we sort of promised each other we wouldn't.

Ann: Tom, a lot has happened since you stepped in the door to-day. You were very observant. I am down to-day, rather raw and fragile. Nevertheless, let's get down to work, and see how we feel at the end of the hour. In order to do this, I'd like you close you eyes, (he does so) and go back to your original feeling, "I just want to hold you."

At last the focussing of the client begins again. I am now back to my original decision. Several other possibilities have presented themselves but under stress (which I am), I return to the first feeling of the hour. It is most often the most fertile to explore.

Tom: Okay. (lengthy pause)

Ann: Just stay with that feeling Tom, and follow where it takes you. (Long pause)

Tom: Ali and I had a fight this week. I didn't like myself in it. I got really pissed off and yelled. It was crazy. (Eyes fly open)

Here I do not know how his feeling of wanting to hold me has led to the fight incident with Ali, but I trust this process and that there is a connection. Thus I decide not to go with the anger but to ask him to close his eyes and follow the images and feelings he has.

Ann: Close your eyes, Tom, and tell me what happened.

Tom: Well, see I was giving Ali a bath and washing her. It was a sexual turn on for me and all of a sudden she starts to cry. I say to her, "Ali, tell me just some little thing that I can do right now to make you happy." And she exploded. She got so mad, telling me about all my unavailability. She is finding that my new job takes too much time away from her. She is not sure that I love her. Whenever she sees you, Ann, she gets very despondent.

Ann: That's true, Tom, she is feeling for the first time that her parents giving her all those material gifts really didn't give her the nurture she needed.

Tom: Well, I am ashamed of myself for getting so angry, but hell, I was trying to care for her. I didn't like it when she cried. I stomped out of the bathroom . . . the whole evening was a write off. I felt angry and I didn't understand Ali's responses.

For me as counsellor there are many choices at this point as I attempt to focus Tom and keep him working. There is his obvious anger which leads him to stomp out of the bathroom, a familiar response in Tom. There is my knowledge of Ali's pain as she attempts to get through to Tom with her need. There is my own difficult space, my needs of the moment. And there is my commitment that Tom's feelings of wanting to hold me have somehow led him to recall with feelings his fight with Ali. Perhaps, stubbornly I decide to endeavour to help Tom find the connection between his wanting to hold me and Ali in the bathtub, because I trust there is a connection.

Ann: I might be able to help with that, Tom. I'd like you to put yourself in the bathtub. Be Ali. Take your time and really try to get into Ali and her feelings. Be her. What are you feeling?

Tom: (as Ali) Sad, really confused about whether to take the new pressure job they are offering me at the office. Do I really want to climb the success ladder like Tom and my Dad?

Ann: What do you want, Ali?

Tom: I want Tom to cheer me up and make all the pain go away. (Tom answers quickly and without feeling.)

Ann: Ali, how do you really feel?

Tom: Down, miserable.

Ann: Stay with that . . . really let yourself feel that down . . . that miserable feeling. (pause) When you are that down, Ali, what is it that you want?

Tom: To forget it and get on with something else.

Ann: Whose voice does that sound like?

Tom: My own! (Tom smiles with recognition)

Ann: It does to me too. Stay with Ali and her despondency. Be that. Try to get right into the centre of it. What do you want for yourself right now, Ali?

Tom: (voice cracking) I just want to be held. I want to cry. (tears start)

Tom's need is awakened here in a powerful way. Tom does not cry easily, and at this point there is sobbing as he feels his need to be held. With this comes the insight that if he reached out and held Ali when she felt sad, his own sadness and hurt would surface. Also the connection with his desire to hold me begins to focus.

Ann: Stay with that feeling as long as you can.

Tom: (Tears come, a long pause . . . eyes fly open) Shit, Ann, I can't do that. I can't hold her. I can't let her hurt. If I did, I'd cry too.

Ann: And that would be a bad idea?

Tom: Come on! We'd be two adults crying in the bathtub! (laughter)

Ann: Well, you'd both be being real, and the evening might have ended differently. (pause) Well, Tom, what is happening inside right now?

Tom: I don't want women to hurt. I want to fix it up. Ah, that's what I wanted to do with you to-day. I wanted to hold you and stop you from hurting. I wanted to stop Ali from hurting in the tub. If I let the hurt happen, I hurt too, and I cry.

Ann: Do you know why, Tom?

It is a poor question, and all counsellors are taught this. I need a question here that would facilitate more completely the connection. "What could feeling sexual have done to my sad feelings at the beginning of the hour?" would have been an interesting possibility.

Tom: No, not for sure. It makes me want to cry when a woman hurts and cries. I might lose control if I didn't try to stop it in some way.

Ann: And?

Tom: That's not a very productive idea.

Ann: Our time is almost used up. It would be easy to go on working, but I promised that we would check at the end of the hour and see how we feel about the session.

Tom: In some ways I feel better. I'd like to know more about what turns me onto a women and how to handle it. It sure does happen to me. Maybe this is a place that I can work on that.

Ann: Tom, I hope so. I'll try to make a safe place. You should know that I do not go to bed with clients. It would be ripping ourselves off. However whatever you feel is data for us to work on.

Tom: That's neat about you. You are one place, one person that accepts everything about me. But how is Ali going to feel? Should I tell her?

Ann: You know, Tom, that I won't.

Tom: Yeah, I know.

Ann: What do want to do?

Tom: I'd like her to know. I'd like to explore the whole issue with her. It must happen to her too. She is one helluva attractive woman.

Ann: That she is, Tom. I'd like her to know too. But, Tom, it won't be easy for her to hear. Perhaps the three of us could look at it together.

Tom: Well, I'll see how it feels. I don't know yet. (pause) I do know that I'd like to know more about myself in the area of women. It has been a life long problem for me.

Tom has been encouraged in this hour to stay with his feelings for me which he experiences as sexual, and in the process has learned about himself. There is the beginning of a connection. There is a moment of really experiencing his own need to be held. At the end there is a clearer focussing of his one 'life long problem' that is centred in his feelings about women.

What if we had tumbled onto the floor into the revelry and ecstacy of sexual expression? In my mind there is no question that we would both have lost immeasurably in who we truly are. I would simply have allowed Tom and myself to repeat neurotic patterns of behaviour.

This verbatim exposes difficulties in which a pastor struggles as she tries to facilitate a client in the difficult area of sexual feelings. Yet it also illustrates the possibilities for growth that exists when the path to honour and explore whatever the client is feeling is pursued with dedication.

This paper concludes having given public hearing to a topic more comfortably kept hidden. The data from my own case load as a female pastoral counsellor and the encouragement of my peers have led me to open the discussion by sharing my own approach to the presence of sexual feelings within the counselling relationship. My approach welcomes dialogue and change.

1. William H. Masters and Virginia E. Johnson. *Human Sexual Inadequacy.* (Boston: Little Brown and Co., 1970).
2. Throughout this paper I will use the term pastor as inclusive of pastors and pastoral counselors.

3. Giavanni Boccaccio, *The Decameron,* Vol, I, (London), p. 43.
4. John Money in *Ethical Issues in Sex Therapy and Research,* edited by William H. Masters, *et.al.* (Boston: Little Brown, 1977), p.169.
5. Sharon Butler and Seymore L. Zelen, "Sexual Intimacies between Therapists and Patients." *Psychotherapy: Theory, Research and Practice* Vol. 14, # 2, Summer, 1977.
6. Charles L. Rassieur. *The Problem Clergymen Don't Talk About.* (Philadephia: Westminister Press, 1976), p.21.
7. John Money, *op cit.,* p. 170.
8. Suan Brownmiller. *Against Our Will.* (Bantom, 1978), p.271.
9. John Money, *op cit.,* p.171.
10. Don S. Browning. *The Moral Context of Pastoral Care* (Philadelphia, Westminster Press, 1976), p.106.
11. *Pastoral Psychology,* June, 1960. p. 49.
12. Butler and Zelen, *op. cit.,* p. 142.
13. Helen Singer Kaplan, *The New Sex Therapy* (New York: Brunner Mazel, 1974), p. 243.

Part Two

Social Transformation

CHAPTER IV

The Church and Latin American Community Development

BY ROY H. MAY, JR.

Increasingly Latin American churches, either as missions still connected with North American or European denominations and independent missionary groups or as autonomous national institutions, are seeking to be engaged in some form of community development. There is an urgency about that involvement. In spite of all the money, technology, and expertise, the gap is growing between rich and poor, not only among nations but within poor countries themselves. As the church becomes involved in community development, it must remember that that involvement truly is an evangelical involvement. Jesus came preaching the Good News to the poor, liberation to the captives, sight to the blind, freedom to the oppressed, and that God's kingdom was at hand. The church's participation in community development must be nothing less than participation in that liberating Gospel.

I. THE PROBLEM

The problem addressed in this paper is that too often involvement of the church is not engagement for liberation, that is genuine development, either in methodology or in conceptual understanding. For the most part involvement has been relief or charity that meets immediate and short-term needs (with high visibility for the benefit of donor constituencies), leaving to others longer involvement that seeks to create new patterns and structures of life. Likewise, programs of churches having more creative involvement are heavily dependent on foreign money and personnel. Church involvement is characterized by varying degrees of paternalism, top-down planning and organization, and outside control whether by missionaries, national church leaders, or donor agencies. Most notable is the absence of serious engagement with social-political structures and institutions, and organization leading to empowerment.

By understanding community development as a neutral, evolutionary process in which education and technical assistance leading to "modernization" viewed as solutions to the problems of the poor, churches and other agencies have missed the fundamental cause of poverty. They have failed to recognize how underdevelopment is related to social-political structures and institutions of injustice characterized by the domination and control of power elites. Even when that relationship has been recognized, it has not been seen as within the province of community development.

Unless development deals intentionally with social-political structures and institutions and seeks to empower people so that they transform, rather than reform or improve present reality, underdevelopment will persist.

The church must re-think its participation in community development. Therefore this paper is directed to those who have responsibility for planning, administering, and evaluating their church's involvement in development, as well as to those in other places who ask, and are asked, to fund that effort. First, a brief definition of development is presented. Then follows a more complete discussion of community development as the process whereby oppressed people discover for themselves their own oppressed condition, their capacity to take power and transform reality, and participate intimately in the actual creation of the new. Specifically, this process will be presented as a three fold, interrelated dynamic of community conscientization, self-reliance, and organization for empowerment. A case study in development will be the vehicle for launching the discussion of that dynamic. Finally, since development traditionally is done by community development agents and organized around specific projects, there will be a brief discussion of how this process might affect the meaning of "projects" and the role of agents. Hopefully, then, this paper will help stimulate that re-thinking of development and offer a concrete framework in which to do it.

It should be explained that this discussion grows out of the author's experience as a United Methodist missionary to Bolivia where he has responsibilities for the analysis and evaluation of Methodist involvement in community development.

II. Meaning of Development

Development is not primarily economic improvement, although that is an important goal, nor is it integration into existing systems of dominance-dependence. Both would defeat the church's concern for social justice and values other than material. Taking seriously New Creation, the goal must be a radical break with the present, unjust order through a process whereby people themselves are empowered to build communities characterized by changing relationships of dominance-dependence to ones of respect, equality, and solidarity. It is the creation of new cultural, political, and economic patterns and conditions that enhance dignity, critical consciousness, and interpersonal communication and cooperation based on the principles of participation and community self-determination. Development does not mean *having* more, but fundamentally *being* more in terms of the quality and relationships of life that emerge from a community's own cultural tradition. Theologically community development can be symbolized by the Old Testament concept of *shalom*, and the New Testament concept of *koinonia*. These two words point to the fullness and wholeness of community, and to an understanding of persons as God's partners in creation.

III. A Case Study in Development

A recent evaluation of two church related development projects in Brazil's Northeast illustrate that not every approach to community development empowers and liberates.

It especially underscores community conscientization and self-reliance. The purpose of the evaluation not only was to analyze a particular project in relation to another and draw conclusions for that project's future, but also to formulate a new policy for development assistance for Brazil's Ecumenical Service Commission.

From all appearances Gurupi, a colonization project, should have been successful. Over a thirteen year period some $1,500,000 of international agency money was invested and nearly a hundred specialized personnel were involved. The basic planning and implementation decisions were made by trained specialists. Yet after a decade it was a failure. Stated project goals had not been met; self-sufficiency, which was to have come within three years, was not in sight. Colonists' morale was low.

On the other hand, the Damasio Project, the improvement of a small town populated by descendents of slaves, received only $8,000 during eight years as a project, no equipment other than axes and shovels, and only four or five personnel, mainly priests and nuns who concentrated in community conscientization rather than improvement projects. Nevertheless the community exhibited a sense of purpose and committment to its future, homes and a school built by the community itself, and the feeling that its problems could be solved.

According to prevailing development theory Gurupi should have been a success and Damasio a failure. Why was that not the case?

The study indicates that success-failure was determined according to the degree that conscientization and self-reliance formed the basis of the development process. In Gurupi, "It had become a well-to-do project, for poor families which, as beneficiaries in the project, remained on the sidelines of decisions made by local agencies or national and foreign bodies."[2] In Damasio, however, the community itself was responsible for analysis, decision, and implementation.

This difference, and its importance, is illustrated by each project's school. Illiteracy in both places is very high, but the evaluators found a marked difference in each community's attitude toward its school. In Gurupi virtually all answers to the evaluators' questions concerning the importance of the school were negative, although the project plan called for a "model primary school for the rural environment." The three qualified teachers, salaried by the state government, had been released.

Only a first grade functioned. As with other aspects of the project, the evaluation reports that "the school was created by the project free of charge and effort...Here the settlers depend entirely on the project..."[3] and made no effort to change.

In Damasio, however, where the school came about by the inhabitants' own decision and effort, interest was high. It was a center of community life, and required their personal involvement and sacrifice, including financial.

Other aspects of the evaluation reveal important differences in the development processes. For instance, in answer to the question, "What kind of aid is most effective?," the majority of Gurupi people identified things they had been given, such as financial assistance, the health program, and their plot of land. Damasio residents pointed to things they had done together, such as community housing, "working in groups," and "our development" answers indicating community solidarity and self-reliance.

Answering the question,"How can you get what is still lacking?" over half the Gurupi community pointed to outside institutions, while in Damasio there was the conviction that solutions to problems rested with the town itself. "The awakening of consciousness among the people of Damasio led them to a state of independence from agencies and outsiders," the report concludes.[4]

Another finding is important. In interviews with surrounding communities, the team of evaluators discovered that Gurupi had had very little influence on them; as a project it offered nothing that could be copied without massive outside intervention. On the other hand, Damasio had greatly influenced other villages, stimulating them in their own development efforts.

Although there are important sociological differences between these two communities as well as other dynamics in the success-failure of the two, the evaluation would seem to support the importance of community conscientization, and self-reliance as the basis of the development process.

IV. Conscientization

The Damasio experience shows that people must be involved integrally in generating and carrying out the development effort. If that is to happen, community conscientization, that is critical analysis and awareness of community problems and the forces impinging on those problems, and the building of trust and solidarity while taking action on the world, is a crucial focus of the community development process.

A theoretical and practical approach for building community conscientization into the development process is that of Brazilian educator Paulo Freire. This approach puts in motion a process of problem-posing discussion through small groups organized for that purpose or utilizes already existing groups such as congregations, Bible studies, Farmer's Cooperatives, Neighborhood Boards, Health Committees, school parents associations, mothers' clubs, and others.

Discussion focuses on the community's own situation as perceived by the group, based upon immediate felt needs. With the help of a community development facilitator, over time the analytical process becomes more and more complex. The various dimensions of felt-needs and community situations are explored more deeply, especially in relation to social-political factors. These felt-needs and community situations are "coded" or objectively represented by a photograph, drama, etc., and posed as contradictions and problems that challenge and require response, not only intellectually but in action.

Freire's concept of conscientization is founded upon several basic assumptions important to the community development process. It is assumed that community people understand their own situation better than anyone else, and that even if illiterate, have the analytical resources to evaluate and determine courses of action. It is assumed that conscientization is a community process and that it occurs only if the facilitator understands himself or herself as no more than an equal among equals whose job is not to give answers, but to ask questions and challenge assumptions. It also assumes that authentic learning and change never can be imposed by people "who know better" but occurs when people themselves deal with their own felt-needs in the context of their own communities. Conscientization comes about as people are able to frame their questions and analysis with greater clarity, see more subtle and complex relationships, and relate to each other in a community process of taking action on a problem.

Reflection-action are two sides of the same process. As Freire writes, "thought has meaning only when generated by action upon the world."[5] Which begins the process will depend upon multiple factors, mainly where people are already in the reflection-action process. What is important is that all action be coupled with reflection and all reflection be joined with action. Thus when action confronts "brick walls," reflection will clarify what is happening and why, and reveal new courses of action.

Conscientization, then, is not a state achieved but a constant process of reflection on engagement.

In a crowded urban neighborhood in Santa Cruz, Bolivia, a small group of workers entered this process as they analyzed scripture passages presented as codes of contemporary situations. The group met weekly for several months with notable changes in the members' ability to analyze their reality. For instance, they moved from blaming others for their poverty to looking at themselves. In a discussion of Amos' famous demands for justice, the group lamented how they were the victims of injustice because "the mayor and big shots don't care about us." But one member suddenly had a new insight, "Maybe it's our own fault because we haven't done anything ourselves," he said. That insight moved the discussion to a new critical dimension.

Another time, as we discussed various passages in Matthew, Luke, and 1st John about loving your neighbor, the group reviewed its social-political reality in terms of those passages.

"To love each other means all are equal, but we're not. We ought to be but in practice, no."

"But that's not the way it should be. Jesus wants a society of equals."

"Well the rich people and the military aren't going to change things because they worry only about their own interests. To them we are just Indians."

"You know," said a young peasant woman who could neither read nor write, "there are two classes of people here, a small class of rich people, and a big class of poor ones—us, and those two classes are in total conflict."

The discussion took an important new direction.

"I think Jesus wants us to make some changes," someone said.

"Well that's a good idea, but we are few in number. We can't do anything," came the all too common reply. Immediately a young construction worker answered with the confidence of Christian hope and added a new dimension to an old verse.

"No, señora, because the Bible says that when two or three are gathered in his name, Jesus is present. We can."

Following meetings dealt with that passage and the empowering presence of Jesus and what that might mean in terms of community organization. We coupled one of those sessions with Matthew 23. 11-12: "The greatest one among you must be your servant. Whoever makes himself great will be humbled and whoever humbles himself will be made great." Here they saw the possibility of a reversal of the present social order, but most importantly came the recognition expressed by one member, "We have to agree and work together because you can't have what's good unless everybody has it. You can't have it alone." In a society where survival often means looking out for yourself, that was an important discovery. It is this kind of intentional discussion that can bring about new awareness of reality and lead to action.

Conscientization means broad community participation in the development effort. Generally, however, participation has meant male participation, with women marginalized from the reflection-action process. The church's involvement in development must take seriously the participation of women, not only for reasons of justice, but because they are vital community members! In fact, many community issues are primarily women's concerns. In Bolivia, for instance, peasant women are in charge of the home, handle family finances and much of the marketing, and have an integral role in farming. Yet how few development projects are directed to women to strengthen them in these very roles, much less to allow them to create new ones. Churches must involve women in the development process, including recruiting and training them as well as men as community development specialists and involving them as the church plans, analyzes, and evaluates its development efforts.

To question an emphasis on women in development in a "machismo" society is to overlook the important roles women do have, and the reality that within their own groups women often express deep dissatisfaction with their exclusion from education and development concerns, and more significant participation in decision-making. This is the growing experience of the Evangelical Methodist Church in Bolivia where peasant women, allied with the few urban women members, are struggling for a greater voice in church affairs, and have pressured the church to committing itself to women's concerns as a major program emphasis, and to their representation on all committees and decision-making bodies. What is important is that development efforts strengthen women in present roles, and allow them opportuities to evolve new ones as vital participants in their communities.

Participation is not new to development literature, but experience shows that those discussions have remained theoretical, and the participation sought is too often a subtle form of manipulating people into accepting already decided upon programs. As in the Gurupi community, how often community needs are determined and projects planned by a church commission or foreign service agency, presented to a community, and carried out under the• agency's or commissions's direction through its technical representative. Basically people are seen as objects who must be helped, and who must be "motivated" or "conscientized" to support the help effort. Genuine participation, however, as the Damasio experience shows is required, means that grass roots people are actively and profoundly involved in discovering their own needs, finding solutions, and carrying out and supporting the whole development process.

V. Self-Reliance

Self-reliance also is emphasized by the valuation of the Gurupi-Damasio projects. The people of Damasio relied largely upon their own efforts to develop their community, whereas Gurupi depended on others. The difference is immediately apparent in terms of financial assistance. It is also evident in the way in which the development process unfolded in each community.

In church circles, the Indian economist and consultant to the World Council of Churches, Samuel L. Parmar, has been the foremost proponent of self-reliance. As he argues, self-reliance does not necessarily mean self-sufficiency or independence from all outside resources. Rather, self-reliance means "optimum use of the resources at hand without denying that other resources might be needed."[6] For him "optimum use of resources at hand" is a fundamental principle of economics. Not to be self-reliant is to waste resources, not to use them at all or at least not to utilize them fully. Reliance on outside assistance indicates a nation or community has not taken seriously the possibilities of its own resources. Thus "self-reliance starts with a decision within a society, country, or group, as to their priorities and their primary needs, and a determination to mobilize their own resources to meet those primary needs and not bring in possible help from outside."[7] Self-reliance requires the decision to be self-reliant, even to the point of refusing assistance.

Too often the process is the reverse. The dependency system means that the first questions asked is, "How much can we get and for what?" When that question is answered, priorities and projects are established. As Parmar says, "once the funds come reliance would be on funds rather than on the spirit and motivation and the drive of the people themselves."[8]

For missionaries and others accustomed to designing development projects requiring international funding, a different orientation will be difficult. Certainly for very poor people it will be difficult to say "no." For both missionaries and community people it will be difficult to discover their own resources, largely because "resources" have been defined almost solely in economic and technological terms. Yet surely the poeple's own creativity and imagination, motivation and hopes, their ability to analyze their own problems, their labor, time, and organization, and even among very poor people, their money, are significant resources that can be stimulated. If these resources do not have primary consideration in planning and administering projects, then there is a great waste as the Damasio: Gurupi experience shows so clearly.

However, self-reliance is hardly a characteristic of Latin American society, certainly not Bolivian society. Dependency is rooted in Spanish colonialism and feudal landholding patterns imposed by Spanish minorities that today effectively are exploited by power elites, both new and old.

Nevertheless, to see the patrón system, as it is known, as essential at least to Andean culture is to overlook the traditional strong spirit of independence, self-government and self-reliance of Indian communities. The patrón system was imposed harshly upon them, and became their means of self-protection when relating to an imposed, external reality. For that same reason, poor people whether Indian, Spanish, or Mestizo, have continued the system to this day. Likewise, Spanish colonial policy was to exploit, not invest. Manufacturing and trade were expressly prohibited in the American colonies. They were to be economically dependent on Spain.

Unwittingly churches have re-inforced the patrón system and patterns of dominance-dependence by placing the center of decision-making and funding not with the people themselves, but with the missionary, the church's central office, and overseas agencies. To change that pattern and follow a policy of self-reliance will be to restore a dignity stolen from the people over 400 years ago.

As a community development principle, it is vital, then, that the locus of decision-making and program support shift from the mission agency or central church office to local communities themselves. Through local and district level church organizations, development programs can be written and passed on to the mission agency or church office for further definition, clarification, technical assistance, and to become part of an integrated approach to development. The experience of the Evangelical Methodist Church in Bolivia, although rudimentary, shows that when given the opportunity and urged to do so, communities are capable of formulating projects. When the emphasis shifted to people's own planning, the church almost was swamped with projects conceived on the local and district levels, many very good, others not so good, and all in need of clarification and definition. Nevertheless it is evident that people can indeed analyze their needs and conceive solutions.

Such a policy clearly has implications for administration. Too often administration of church development projects is complex and bureaucratic, requiring technocratic skills few illiterate people possess. For example, although the Evangelical Methodist Church in Bolivia urged local groups to formulate their own projects, a constant frustration of the Project Planning and Evaluation Committee was the form in which project proposals were presented. The Committee circulated a form-sheet showing how projects should be written, but it was never used. The principal designers of the form, however, were highly trained in United States and Argentinian universities with additional study in project planning in the national university's department of economics. No wonder local people did not use the Committee's outline! Administration must be clear and simple.

Likewise self-reliance requires that technological innovation be simple, accessible, and easily duplicated. This too is illustrated by the Damasio-Gurupi evaluation. Technology must be appropriate to the capacity and resources of the people, and coherent with the traditional technology it replaces. Tractors may seem to be the obvious answer to increased production, but are tractors simple machines, easily accessible to the majority of peasant people, and can they be duplicated by others? What about the cost and quality of maintenance, to say nothing of spare parts? What ramifications might tractors have on the people's social-cultural traditions? Technology must be appropriate to the situation.

Conscientization and self-reliance do not mean romanticizing and labelling as totally correct all decisions made at the local level, as Julio de Santa Ana, the Uruguayan consultant on development to the World Council of Churches, reminds us. "Instead," he says, "there should be an effort to create conditions for the existence of true solidarity on the basis of which any project drawn up is done so in mutual, co-responsible fashion, and as a response to human needs. This means that those providing financial, technical, or personnel aid must view as problems what in the view of the project planners are their problems."[9] Development, he says, is a partnership venture. Partnership means that development is a dialogue between the local level where underdevelopment is lived and the "central office" which has responsibility for finding the resources and technical support that may be needed. It then no longer is a "top-down" approach, but "both ways" based on the principles of participation and self-reliance.

VI. Organization For Empowerment

Historically, in every Latin American country where significant social-structural change has occured, it has resulted from well organized pressure. As Dutch sociologist Gerrit Huizer has noted of groups pressuring for land reform, "Sometimes these activities have been within the possibilities and procedures of the law, sometimes they were acts of civil disobedience, at the margin or in circumvention of the law, sometimes against it."[10] The important point is that it was organized pressure that forced changes. If development is serious about social-structural change, then organization for empowerment must be an integral part of the process.

Organization for empowerment has revolutionary potential in that it changes class relationships. First, it requires power elites to deal with the oppressed as equals, and secondly, the oppressed themselves realize they are equal and not inferior, that they are their own "patron." Feelings of impotence turn into potential, and a new self-image and class consciousness emerge. A third factor is that organization means political power. For structural change to occur, these three potentials are essential. *Organized* power is important because it means strength in solidarity and because it can prevent people's action from becoming nothing more than "sporadic and directionless agitation,"[11] as Parmar warns. Without question in Latin America organizational effort is a delicate process, and open efforts will meet severe resistance. Action must shift from highly visible efforts to a silent ministry of grass roots organization.

Thus the small grass roots community group has vital importance, but its strength is not in itself. It is in linking it with other groups, large and small, to form formal and informal networks of grass roots organizations. That must be an intentional part of the community development process.

The church is in a particularly strategic position to promote that kind of organization for empowerment. Congregations, Bible study groups, women's societies, and social action projects in every neighborhood and throughout the countryside are ready made community groups to be networked together. In addition they have a national organization to support them and facilitate communication at other levels. Most importantly, especially under repressive regimes, churches have a certain legitimacy that political, labor, and student organizations do not have. Churches can organize when other groups cannot. This is not to say the church has no difficulties; it is only to suggest that it has leverage that other groups do not have and that it can use that leverage as a resource to promote organization for empowerment.

The grass roots communities project of Latin American Catholics offers a model. Throughout their large parishes, both urban and rural, priests have promoted the formation of small groups of parishioners to study the Bible, pray, and discuss issues vital to them. These groups are networked with each other through the priest, and communication occurs through the daily and Sunday mass, as well as parish wide activities. Although their purpose is not expressly political, many have become a political force. In Brazil where they are best organized and supported, especially in urban areas, they are becoming a source of pressure which the government cannot ignore and are deepening the conflict between church and state over such issues as human rights and the welfare of the poor.

Organization for empowerment is not something done as a separate project. It is an intentionality that underlies all community development effort, whether the focus is health, education, or agricultural production. It becomes a part of every project. A cattle improvement program would concern itself also with peasant farmer organization so that they themselves plan, direct, and support the project, and in turn are networked with similar projects. That networking might not be primarily "political." It may well be "only" to facilitate distribution of vaccines and access to technical assistance. Nevertheless, it also will be organization for empowerment. The same can be done with health committees and mothers clubs. What must be realized is that networking does not just happen; it is made to happen.

If social-political structures and institutions are to be dealt with seriously by empowering the poor, then the church must be serious about organization, about networking its many grass roots groups and projects.

VII. Implications For Projects and Agents

As Latin American churches begin to understand community development in the terms discussed here, the role of the community development agent or missionary will change. Instead of having the role of imparting knowledge, it will be to dialogue with local communities, to push them for deeper questioning about their reality and for clarification of what they are saying, and facilitate its decisions through contacts and technical expertise. Certainly he or she must offer alternatives and present their own views. It is important that if one's training and experience suggest a community's plan is incorrect and will not work or that other alternatives might be preferable, the worker must say so. Yet in so doing one must remember, as Paulo Freire says, "It is not our role to speak to the people about our own view of the world, nor to attempt to organization for empowerment. Above all it will require deepened faith in the abilities of local people and that their efforts will have an impact far beyond the boundaries of their neighborhoods and villages.

1. John T. Pawlikowski, "Social Ethics: Biblical and Theological Foundations," paper prepared for publication by the regional association of Catholic Bishops in southern Africa, 1977.
2. Waldo A. Cesar, *Toward a New Aid Policy* (Rio de Janeiro: CENPLA-Study, Research and Planning Center, 1974), p. 22.
3. *Ibid.,* p. 37.
4. *Ibid.,* p. 55.
5. Paulo Freire, *Pedagogy of the Oppressed* (New York: Herder and Herder, 1972), p. 64.
6. Samuel L. Parmar, "Focus on the Poor," *Ecumenical Review,* July 1976, p.272.
7. *Ibid.,* p. 274.
8. Samuel L. Parmar, "The Politics of Development," *One World,* July/August 1976, p. 8.
9. Julio de Santa Ana, "What Development Demands: A Latin American Position," in Richard D. N. Dickinson, *To Set at Liberty the Oppressed, Towards an Understanding of Christian Responsibility for DevelopmentLiberation* (Geneva: World Council of Churches, 1975), p. 148.
10. Gerrit Huizer, *Land Reform, Land Settlement, and Cooperatives,* No. 2 (Rome: Food and Agriculture Organization, 1971), p. 1.
11. Samuel L. Parmar, "Issues in the Development Debate," in Dickinson, *To Set at Liberty the Oppressed,* p. 175.
12. Freire, p. 85.
13. *Ibid.,* p. 67.
14. James N. Becht, "Salud, Nutrición y Ambiente y el Papel de la Iglesia en el Dessarrollo," in Consejo de las Iglesias Metodiastas en America Latina, *Consulta sobre el Hambre* (mimeograph), 1976, p. 69.
15. Parmar in Dickinson, *To Set at Liberty the Oppressed,* p. 176.

CHAPTER V

Educating For Freedom

BY RENNY GOLDEN

This paper describes an educational program begun on the West Side of Chicago three years ago which incorporates Paolo Freire's methodology of educating for freedom. The central process employed, conscientization, is a process of liberation. Such a concrete attempt of liberation is, we believe, what we are called to do by God's word. To unfold the theological basis of this ministry of education, I have to explain, therefore, our understanding of God's word. It is influenced by the perspective of liberation theology which can be characterized by the following citation from a lecture of Ricardo Antoncich:

> If the word of God is subversive and if it radically changes the spontaneous values of people (for example, the paradoxical beatitudes which fly in the face of our cultural values), then the theology which is faithful to the subversive character of that work, is also a theology of questioning, of transforming praxis...The praxis of this community is a historical praxis, that is, an experience of faith as a transforming change of the conditions of society; a move from oppressive conditions to conditions of liberty, a radical questioning of the existing order and a search for a new order.[1]

We understand therefore God's word as a subversive word. Subversive, because it reveals the human destiny to be free, because it judges any form of oppression and because it calls and enables to a process of comprehensive liberation.

The Word of God reveals the human destiny to be free. Revelation (in Freire's term: conscientization) allows the oppressed to see the social contradictions that define their lives and impels them to move from being objects of history to being the subjects, from being destined to those who create their own destiny.

The Word of God judges any form of oppression. An important form of oppression today is institutional violence: the violence a poor or oppressed person experiences when they can find no work, when they spend hassled hours at public aide offices, when Cook County Hospital is the only option for their sick children, when woman work as seamstresses in factories for little pay and come home at night to begin family labor, when education socializes them to accept this situation as normal.

This institutional violence is the result of structural systems of relationships and as such is the objectification of the sin of a people. This sin is one in which we all are collectively complicit, for we are part of institutions which imply that some—on the basis of race, nationality, sex or class—deserve more power, resources, rights, etc. than others. Such institutions contradict justice which insures the right to live humanly to all persons; such institutions contradict charity-love which calls us to love others as we love God. Our socio-economic reality is at the same time a religious reality: "Therefore, misery, institutional violence and so forth are not merely problems of temporality but also of salvation."[2]

A form of institutional violence that we are addressing is the educational system. It is this system which the dominant social order employs to justify its vision of reality which maintains an unequal distribution of resources and power. Through our education system people are socialized to accept this specific value system (capitalism) which determines the options and milieu people experience as reality.

The problem we face is that our educational system claims on the one hand to be democratic and just but socializes people to fit a competitive, unjust system. The claim of democracy and the actual economic functioning of such a system are contradictory. The contradictions are difficult to unmask since people are slotted from early in their lives, particularly through education, to believe that the 'American Dream' of freedom for all is true and is their reality and a failure to realize this dream is their fault, when in fact the American dream of democracy does not work on their behalf. Our task then is to provide an opportunity for oppressed people to critically evaluate their educational programming and their own experience in order to discover any contradictions. To discover such contradictions and act to transform the structures (in our case, the educational system) which limit real freedom and democracy, is liberating.

We see our work in the broader context of the struggle for justice for all. We think that the educational system is the most formative institution for maintaining the competitive base which continues to keep the poor and oppressed on the bottom stratum of the society and the rich on top. What is needed is an educational process which seriously engages the aspirations of the oppressed and poor, however initially unfocused, and opts with them to transform the dominant society's oppressive educational system. Such a process, patiently struggled, is liberating.

Before beginning a history and description of our program I wish to make some comments about the limits of such a description. Although an attempt will be made to show how our program incorporates the methodology of Freire, some cautions about the application of this methodology need to be stated.

Freire, a Latin American educator, has set forth a methodology he calls "the practice of freedom" whereby men and women deal critically with their own reality in order to transform it to their own purposes. In a two week seminar spent with Paolo in Pontiac, Michigan he responded over and over again to the frustrated requests of educators and organizers that he explain how his method worked. Paolo's only response was that Americans want a "package" or a "kit" which they can take and apply to a situation and make it work. In keeping with his methodology, he insisted that they had to discover the contradictions in their own situation and act with others to transform these limiting conditions. He could not, he suggested, give *a priori* solution. Further, the essence of his methodology was that *only they* could know their reality and begin the task of reflection and action to overcome the obstacles to human freedom these bounds represented.

In this same way what we offer here is a description, often incomplete, which comes in the form of clues to possibilities. Our reality is ours, and our experience is not transferable for others. We hope the sharing of our experience becomes an impetus or challenge to others, but we are not offering a blueprint. The key is praxis (reflection-action-return to reflection). Freire's work was/is for us an inspiration, but we soon learned to avoid slavish imitation of his methodology since such a decision misunderstands his methodology. For many who read this story a critique will be made more in terms of our *lack of* incorporation of Freire's method than needed crticisms of our work. For others a critique will be leveled against us *because of* our appropriation of Freire's method (Freire critics consider such a process as already limited and lacking in an action component aimed directly at structures of oppression). In both cases we can only respond by encouraging people to judge and evaluate *our work*.

This paper is a description of the journey of some educators who began to be educated by the people who are oppressed by the educational system. It is the story of their (educators) beginning liberation, but most importantly it is the story of people who by their efforts change the hold on their lives of the educational system.

Those of us coming from activist involvement in social change in the past understood the need for liberation and shared such a vision, but didn't know how to engage such a process with marginated people, nor were we clear about the point of entry into such struggle. Similarily as educators we knew *what* was being taught was determinant in terms of oppression or liberation, but we didn't attend to *how* it was being taught. Our first jarring hint of a possible methodology which could liberate was the work of Paolo Freire.

The hope offered by Freire's work was/is both an impetus and a nemesis. Impetus—though we weren't clear on where to begin, Freire's overriding clue to engagement was praxis. If the full reality of that moment wasn't clear to us at first, the imperative to action was. In this sense Freire's work was the inspiration for our beginning. Nemesis—we're still in the process of dymystifying Freire and learning to trust our own experience in a USA urban setting.

With such an impetus to act upon assumptions, our (Joan Jeter and I) awakening began. This awakening catalyzed a beginning dialogue with West side people about their lives, their hopes and dreams. What in society benefited them, what did not, what *is supposed* to benefit *all* and does not? Did education benefit them as poor blacks and latins? For whom did the educational system work? These questions emerged after listening to many stories. Slowly, the questions became part of the story, a weave that yielded a pattern for people, for us.

All the institutions, public aide, the court system, law enforcement and work, surrounding people's lives did not benefit them. They accused surrounding institutions primarily of racism and less clearly recognized discrimination against themselves as poor people. These two oppressions, race and class, were so predominant that few of the women identified the sexist nature of these institutions. Individual people told us of their exploitation and suffering but primarily identified their oppression as the result of racial discrimination. The more we listened and probed, the more the systemic nature (through interstructuring of race, class and sex discrimination) of people's oppression emerged.

That conviction about the systemic nature of oppression reinforced our understanding that culture creates education and that education maintains the ideological support for these institutions. Any education that was liberating, we postulated, would challenge these ideological assumptions that all of us in some ways appropriate. It was no surprise then to learn that the institution of public school education which mediates the dominant culture's system of oppression of poor people, women and races, had failed people years ago when they dropped or were pushed out of high school. Many people felt shame or anger about this and were even angrier or more discouraged about attempts in their adult lives to pass the GED test, the only means of receiving a high school diploma for a high school dropout (GED—Graduate Equivalency Diploma).

In order to understand the alternative nature of our program, an understanding of what we were against is necessary. For this reason a description of the GED program and its effects on people's lives follow. The GED is a national attempt to offer high-school credentials to dropouts. A person wishing to complete their high school education no matter how near or how far from graduation they were when they dropped out of school, need only pass the GED test successfully. The individual enrolled in GED preparation classes may retake the test as often as they wish. The GED test is, according to Latino veterans of such a testing game, an 'anglocized' test; according to blacks it incorporates a white middle class language style, format and context. The GED program not only failed to meet people's needs; it reinforced the alienation and discouragement people were attempting to overcome by taking such a test. The GED is a failure program set up for 'failures' of its base educational system. If the public school system was unsympathetic to the needs of the people originally, the mechanistic indifference of this 'testing machine' program is enormous.

If previous to entering our program, over 40% of those presently enrolled in our program failed to pass the GED test after repeated testing, how effective is such a program that claims to be helping high school dropouts? This program is not neutral—it is designed to continue the stratification of human beings while allowing some determined individuals by its ever narrowing entrée to status in society in order to justify the claim that educational opportunity is equally available to all. This is not to suggest a high school or even college degree is a legitimate entrée to privilege in this society if the recipient is from a racial minority, particularly a minority woman. On the contrary, the structures of the dominant society still discriminate.

Our determination after hearing the people's words was to struggle with them for a transformation of the educational system. Considering the enormity of the task we knew the attempt would be modest but if true to people's reality it would be a faithful beginning. We also knew the answer was not a better product (educational system) but a process that would critically question the experiences of people in those very structures they'd seen as discriminatory.

History Of Program

Concretely, people were asking, at the least, for an alternative to the GED program. They wished a program that would grant an accredited high school diploma but would not be as alienating as the GED. Since we were in dialogue with older and middle aged community members, rather than recent high school drop-outs, emphasis was placed on a need for life experience evaluation as a basis for credit. We were all previously apprised of the state (NCC-North Central Committee) requirement of 16 credits to receive an accredited diploma. This emphasis on life experience valued the rich resources and skills people brought to the program and already began to reverse the 'banking method' (you come to us empty and we will fill you with knowledge) process of public school education.

The critical question for us in attempting initiation of such a program was how do you engage poor marginal city dwellers with such an investment of their lives in one more educational program? One answer was to develop a process like Freire's which would use the resources of the people, a process that would start with their reality, not the educators or staff.

To meet these needs a program was developed with group work (sharing of experiences and a support group for each person's struggle to stay with their educational goals) as the program core. Skills courses, independent study, credit for community organizational involvement were also components of the program. The methodology employed (Freire's) was that the participants generate the themes (curriculum) and determine their own educational goals.

With such a skeletal organizational plan and methodology, Joan Jeter and I, with input from community members, began to develop a staff. We invited two other staff members from the high school we were working in to spend long evening hours helping us strategize and plan. After months of this effort we recognized the need for a team of instructors and salaries to hire them. I approached Tom Heaney of Loop College's Continuing Education Program for funding assistance. I wrote the proposal he suggested and when it was accepted we were ready to hire instructors.

Our next task was to recruit people for the program. Some of those who gave input on the need and type of program envisioned were interested. For the rest, Joan and I, walked the streets of Roosevelt Road talking to local storekeepers about our program. Eventually we recruited 40 people who in January, 1972, began the program in the basement of St. Mary's Center for Learning (the school from whom we rent space). We have not had a recruitment program for almost 2 years. Each semester there is a waiting list of people who wish to attend the program. However, in the first year of the program, particularly with those first recruits, convincing people that we'd do what we said we'd do (grant a high school diploma by offering an alternative to GED) was difficult. From the very beginning the program changed, modified and renewed itself with each new group who challenged or critiqued the process.

The present program, directed by Joan Jeter, has an enrollment of 600 with an additional 500 projected for March, June and September. Our program runs quarterly. Additionally, we have opened a bi-lingual, bi-cultural Latino program in the 18th Street area of the West side.

The Latino satellite program,begun a year ago, is small (45 people) with an all Latino staff. The program has had difficulty beginning. One mistake we made was to exclude spoken English from the program entirely. We believed that many Latinos are discriminated against in terms of employment and education because they don't speak English. Further, young Latins entering our educational system often learn that their language and culture are secondary and less valuable than the dominant language and culture. We wished to reverse this process by offering an educational program leading to a high school diploma exclusively in Spanish by Latino instructors. We postulated that participants would learn English through the numerous 'English as a Secondary Language' programs offered in the community. Further, we wished to avoid making a high school diploma contingent upon learning English, based on the assumption that people would learn English as they perceived the need in order to secure the jobs they felt more eligible for according to their increased educational status. Such assumptions were not checked out enough with the people involved in the program. We had trusted the suggestions of some organizers in the 18th Street community. We failed to do the necessary work of bringing the question to the people, not organizers, who benefit from such a program. Again we were reminded that it is only the people themselves who can create possibilities for liberation because it is only they who experience the oppression.

In the black community and with Latins who are fluent, a high school diploma is perceived initially as a prime need. Whereas Latinos initially perceive fluency in English as their priority. We have accomodated this need in the 18th Street program by offering classes primarily in Spanish (as a number of the participants speak limited English) but with a bilingual approach to content courses, though discussions are usually in Spanish.

The Latin staff believes a distinct advantage to their program, in terms of Freire's methodology, is the single cultural experience their people reflect upon. The main program, which is 85% black, 14% Latino and 1% white ethnic, struggles with a diversified cultural reality. The themes that emerge, however, in the main program are primarily concerned with the black experience but accomodations are made to other experiences.

The other advantage to the 18th Street program is its smaller size and the more intensely communal nature of the program because of its location in one local community and the fact that most of the staff live or work in the neighborhood. The main program on the other hand is city wide, drawing from the black neighborhoods on the West and South sides of the city.

Of the five hundred persons enrolled in our total program approximately 30% are presently or have been involved in drug (mostly methodone maintainence) programs, approximately 45% are on welfare, and the remaining participants range from teacher and community health aides, LPN's for Model Cities, to folks with no visible means of support.

The December graduates of the main program totaled approximately 200. In a year's time approximately 1,000 people were involved in our program. This is a dramatic rise in the program's participants since the program began three years ago with 40 participants. Our dropout rate is the lowest in the city. Of 540 people enrolled last semester, 495 participants completed the semester.

STAFF

Originally a team of four women administered the program, but our funding agency at the time (Loop College of Continuing Education) insisted that a director be appointed. Yielding on that issue was somewhat cooptive for us and has caused innumerable personal and programmatic problems. Personal because the woman who directs our program, Joan Jeter, was thereby placed in a charismatic leadership role with all the pressures that being answerable to a funding and controlling agency can bring. A further pressure was the real problem of being answerable to 500 people at one time. Programmatic, because a hierarchical model was foisted upon us at the administrative level even though our interior administrative staff relationships were mutual in practice. Still such roles strain attempts at mutuality. We still struggle with this contradiction, though the check and balance system operative in the different interest groups in the program subjects all staff, educators, participants and volunteer help to the same evaluation process. The administrative staff (as are participants) is evaluated by the Governing Council, and it may not make school policy decisions.

Other administrative staff members consist of one assistant director, two part-time administrators, two registrars, one secretary, and CEDA trainees who do clerical work.

The administrative staff (and faculty) is primarily black, and the staff-faculty of the 18th Street St. Pius Program is all Latino. The Administrative team in addition to being primarily black was all women. A fact that has caused some conflicts with our primarily male funding agency. More recently a man from our faculty has been working part-time on the administrative team.

There are 63 faculty members in our program. In the main program, the skills or content area instructors are primarily black, except for the Latin instructors on 18th Street; there are two Latino instructors and the remainder are white. All the group facilitators are black except for one white facilitator. We are able to draw faculty from a wide variety of disciplines and backgrounds because our evening program doesn't conflict with day time work commitments.

In addition to faculty drawn from professions and the community, we hire people who have graduated from our program and spent two semesters in a more intensive group training program we offer, to work as group facilitators. In this way we can draw faculty from people who've experienced the process. Usually these group facilitators act as co-facilitators initially.

Decision Making

Participants in the program, alumni, two instructors from the instructors' organization and one administrator comprise the Governing Council which totals about 30 people but numbers can rise to 60 people on certain issues. Here curriculum is approved, teaching and administrative staff are hired or fired and on-going program evaluation is made. Governing Council is a course whose meetings are open to all participants. Members of the Governing Council evaluate classes, rate teachers, consider learner evaluations of their teachers and recommend the teachers' continuation or termination in the program. Any participant is eligible to become a member of the Governing Council simply be registering for the course.

Because many Governing Council members graduate within two semesters there was an initial shifting focus as each new Council was formed. However we discovered that the overall educational process itself provided continuity and further many new people who took part in the council were cousins or friends apprised through the oral tradition of the experiences and function of the previous Council. Further continuity is offered by Administrative Team members, Instructor members and Alumni members (one of whom was part of our first graduating class).

It is important to us to offer the Governing Council as a course because it is congruent with our philosophy that the workings and milieu of the program itself is conscientizing. Also, the experience of responsibility for the program's destiny is empowering for people. And finally it is only the people who know what is best for the people. It is the conviction that only those experiencing oppression can discover the contradictions in their reality and act to transform those obstacles which we've had to return to over and over again as the guiding principle for our actions.

The respect participants hold for their experience as Council members is reflected in the increased return of alumni to membership on this decision making board. And this despite the often long, arduous hours members put into this process. Further, it is the Governing Council who call all school community assemblies to deal either with external pressures from the school we rent space from or funding agency demands. This means they act as enforcers of agreed upon rules such as 'no smoking' or 'eating in classrooms'; also they deal with questions about credits. They are often the group who takes the "flak" when each new group enters the program and questions policy or rules. Finally, they bear a heavy responsibility for decisions to drop members who have failed to attend classes or not rehire or fire faculty or Administrative members. (They are the last appeals board).

The danger of the Council's power grabbing or repeating the model of authority the culture offers is blocked by the different interest groups represented on the Council ie., instructors and administration and most importantly their accountability to the community who will challenge their decisions. We attribute some of the success of the Governing Council on issues of justice to their faithfulness and sensitivity to the people who make up the school community. Another reason for their effectiveness is that some members who seek out such a course do so because they already possess community organization skills and are interested in offering their talents for the community's benefit.

Turning to the mechanics of our program an outline of procedures for entering the program and a statement of purposes and objectives follows.

Current Program Description

Each potential participant is interviewed before registration to determine their goals and expectations and learn about our program. After this interview and a careful review of individual transcript records, work and life experiences, up to two years of credit may be given. Participants then meet with the registrar to determine the number of credits still needed to meet the state requirements of 16 credits to graduate. These credits are earned in a variety of ways.

- —group sessions which increase political and social awareness
- —in-service training with community organizations and agencies
- —independent study
- —weekend residential seminars on urban survival education
- —courses offered in local community colleges
- —teaching a class to peers in concentrations in which the participant has expertise (eg., languages, organizational skills, etc.)
- —special adult courses offered for participants in areas required for graduation, but with special focus on community concerns
- —'mini' workshops that take place on weekends at some resource in the city, eg., science workshop at Museum of Science and Industry, health workshop at a Community Clinic in Lawndale, Holiday Court

Purpose and Objectives

A. to offer an adult education program leading to a high school diploma which will be responsive to the needs of inner-city residents of diverse ethnic and racial backgrounds.

B. to transform a societal hurdle which spells failure to many, eg., a high school diploma, into a meaningful personal, social and educational experience

C. to develop through education the political and social independence of a marginal and poverty community and create within this community the skills necessary to survive in and effect positively their urban environment

D. to develop a process within which adults can experience self affirmation personally and collectively

E. to develop a critical awareness about the educational system

F. to develop an awareness of the city-as-learning resource so that education and life are not polarized in the lives of inner-city minorities and that growth and development can be seen as a life long process

In order to treat the philosophical foundations of our program, a brief return to our chief obstacle in beginning the program will be made. Neighborhood and community people told us what they needed educationally but the greatest block to beginning was fatalism.

Freire speaks of the problem of fatalism which is the result of internalizing the mind of the oppressor; this must be confronted. The fatalistic attitude of oppressed people is quite simply that they are helpless victims and they may as well accept 'reality'. In the same way people we approached simply couldn't believe we wouldn't run out on them as so many government and state experimental programs had done when funding ceased; also their discouragement with GED made them doubt their own ability to ever actually graduate. People had internalized the myths of the public school system; they believed they'd failed the educational system. What was needed was a process that would deeply immerse folks in a critical reflection on their experience that would lead to increased awareness about the *limits* to their social, political and personal reality.

This awareness about reality involves a casting off of social and educational myths and unquestioned value assumptions. When such a struggle and confrontation is engaged in the group it leads to a change in life standpoint or consciousness. People no longer feel as victims but as creators of their own history. Concretely, to recognize you are not a failure or 'dummy' because you lack a high school diploma, but to perceive the educational institution as the failure, is to experience a new freedom, a new sense of worth, a new political awareness. The unmasking of the real failures is what Freire refers to as conscientization.

Group

A process that could lead to conscientization would be a central element in our program. This concept is the core of our program and we refer to the actualizing of this idea as, simply—GROUP. As Paolo Freire states:

> The real problem which people...no matter what their level of knowledge is to become more and more human beings...it must be the effort by which persons at the time in which they think about their presence in the world should be able to learn how to read and write. At the same time...they must overcome their fatalistic attitude with regard to reality and discover that they are capable of transforming the reality which is made by themselves.

Group is, first of all, a support system for participants in the program. Many of our participants work all day, come home from work, prepare a meal for their children, and make it to St. Mary's for night classes from 6 to 10 p.m. four nights a week. Continuing that commitment requires a continual encouragement from fellow and sister members who inspire and care about each other's progress and involvement. The group is not an intensive encounter group nor is it just a 'rap' session. Because of our determination not to separate the personal social-political dimension, group is seen as an opportunity to generate themes about work, family life, urban problems, education housing, etc. (content); but also process skills and group leadership skills are stressed so that an interpersonal dimension is developed.

Without a group process incorporating the interpersonal goals of caring, listening, and giving honest feedback, our program would simply be another more or less alienating attempt of the dominant society's offer of education which fails to connect to the reality of the lives of poor people. Group is a commitment to trust the experiences of the participants in the program. Group actualizes all the intellectual words about the value of the cultural experience of participants.

Conscientization As Function Of Group

To understand education as a process means engagement with the world seen as a constant deep unfolding of historical and cultural experience and a commitment to humanize and liberate it. Through this critical reflective process focused on people's experience, particularly of education, a new consciousness emerges; a throwing off of the educational system's damaging stranglehold. From such "awakening of consciousness" that the group process provides, an understanding vis-a-vis the sharing of others, of the social nature of all learning takes place. The inital conviction that all learning is social is reinforced by the *common* discovery of past alienating educational experiences.

The stimulus for conscientization derives from interpersonal dialogue in which people discover the meaning of humanness. This process begins a journey taken by educators and participants alike which breaks thru oppressive educating by changing the sojourners historical situations and relationships. The praxis (practice) of living out the new relationship between educator and participants lifts up a new possibility which expunges the internalized hierarchical model of teacher-expert vs. student-novice model. The group praxis becomes one of mutuality and cooperation as opposed to the dominant educational model of individual achievement and competition. Further, group action around school issues, decisions and problems takes place.

Conscientization does not have as its goal a predictable direction. Critics of a program such as ours accuse us of creating rebels or socialists (unfortunately we're far from that successful). This is a misunderstanding of the process; if social-political dissatisfaction is the result of the group dialogue it is because that is the reality people experience. To engage a process of reflection/action/reflection is political because the contradictions in the human situation people discover are political. In this sense the method we use is subversive since our intent would be to subvert an unchanging social order in order to create new possibilities. Our ideological (value assumptions) would be that people should be free to choose their own destinies and not be mainpulated by an educational system that limits those choices and systematically 'slots' people according to race, sex and class position.

Group is a crucible for change and growth. Most content and skills courses in our program also employ a group process approach to learning. The course called GROUP, however, has the sole objective of initiating a critical questioning approach to reality as a means of personal and political transformation. The group experience is the foundation on which our entire program hinges.

A final question we are asked about group is simply "How do you begin such a process and what have your mistakes taught you?" We have no formula and to say we let what will happen, happen is considered a 'cop-out' by inquirers. Yet the essence of the methodology is an act of trust in people's willingness to share with each other and to discover the common nature of their experience. A belief in this *will* to move out of isolation, toward community and deeper self understanding and self realization is what group facilitators bring to their groups. Some response to questions about the purpose of group or a sharing of the facilitators experience in groups is offered at the beginning of group. This style of beginning, however, is different for each facilitator. What is common is an initial simple discussion about group. After that people often engage many different themes such as; work, family, race, sex, public aide, prison experience, drugs and alcoholism. Many of the group goals that emerge from the group contracting process are as follows:

A. to develop a support system by creating an atmosphere of trust

B. to see education as a process rather than a product

C. to emphasize the importance of group learning

D. to understand that learning means change intellectually, emotionally, and socially-politically

E. to offer the model of the teacher as facilitator, not an instiller of knowledge

F. to offer the model of the teacher or facilitator as co-learner who is not responsible for another's learning

G. to develop feedback skills and accurate confrontations so that group members can interact equally

H. to develop co-responsibility and accountability among group members

I. to develop an understanding that the very process of learning being experienced in group and class is social-political and must be opened to scrutiny by the entire group

J. to develop critical awareness; critical questioning about reality

Contract and Course Evaluation

All courses and groups in the program are required to have a written contract signed by all members of the course/group which states the goals of that group. This decision was reached by the Governing Council to provide an evaluation tool (the group goals become the evaluation criterion at the end of the course) for faculty participants and Governing Council members. Since all our courses rely upon process and consensus decision, the process of arriving at a group contract places responsibility on all members while engaging the group upon its initial meeting in the sometimes arduous task of working out a collective decision. This process, often difficult for new participants and new teachers in the program, replaces the 'banking method' approach (in which the teacher as expert tells you what you need to learn) with a process which encourages people to express what they want to learn. The contracting process energizes the group members to say what their goals are and recognize the thematic (social nature) of mutual needs while respecting requests of individuals. We avoid making individual contracts between teacher/and student because this procedure reinforces the individualistic, isolated and competitive model of education we're attempting to transform. Course evaluation is done by all members verbally and though we don't use grades but a written evaluation, a member might be judged to have not passed or completed a course by the group. The written evaluation, which reflects the groups evaluation, is the responsbility of the staff member of that course. In certain skills courses the input during the evaluation process falls more heavily upon the instructor and the individual member than on the entire group.

Courses

Courses range from an economics course 'Blood, Sweat and Money', and social studies course 'Black and Brown in the Red, White and Blue' to 'Kung Fu' and 'Parent Effectiveness Training'. Several weekend seminars which rely upon the city as resource provide participants with an opportunity to experience and critique certain institutions. An example of this is a course called 'Criminal Justice' which meets at Holiday Court of the Juvenile Court or Adult Court. After viewing several trials the group meets to critique and discuss the implications of the judicial system's functioning and its relationship to their lives as blacks and latinos. Other seminars such as the 'Mural Painting weekend' visit city murals, and the participants completed a mural of their own under the direction of R. Patlan, an artist who studies Mural Painting in Mexico.

The group process whereby all members act as resource persons for other group members is incorporated in all courses, including skills courses such as math, science, typing etc. The objective is to facilitate the group members' understanding of the collective learning process as well as paying attention to individual needs in skills areas. As new members come into a course there is an initial tendency to expect the instructor to tell people what they will learn. This is because people's only experience of learning has been an internalized 'banking method' whereby the 'teacher' tells you what you need to know. Each instructor must resist this temptation. Often members accuse the instructors in initial class sessions of not doing anything and challenge them to do what they're being paid for, eg., 'teach us'. This challenge to the instructor comes as an attack on their competency from a consciousness that has internalized the mind of the oppressor. When such challenges are met and the responsibility for learning is placed in the group rather than instructor, a new milieu is created. In this atmosphere participants are freed up to identify the skill areas they wish to pursue. It usually amazes people, when engaging in this critical self evaluation process, *that they know more than they thought.*. Confidence to pursue their goals comes not only from the common discovery of problems but also the common discovery of successes. Members who have greater understanding of some levels of a specific skill act as resource persons to other members. The instructor initially coordinates this process, owns her or his own expertise, and makes her or himself available to small working groups or individuals who wish advice. All skills areas, by responding to the expressed practical needs of participants, are related to the daily lives of members. Math, for example is taught in terms of percentages of mortgages, or percentages of black workers in blue collar, white collar jobs, interest on bank loans, income tax form computation etc.

Funding – Can Public Monies Be Used For Radical Education?

Our program was originally funded by a small grant of state funds through the Loop College Continuing Education Program. Since that time our funding still comes from state monies to the ICCB Illinois City College Board. The Skills Center which is part of the city college program funds us as an adult alternative high school. To say there's been tension between ourselves and the Skills Center is like saying the Arabs and Israelies have a slight communication problem.

Often it has seemed that we were speaking different languages. We have not naively put down the disagreements to a communication or vague philosophical difficulty. On the contrary the question emerges over and over and over for us—can public monies be used for radical education? The problem is complex and space doesn't permit a full discussion of the pros and cons of this issue. Our experience tells us that you continue the program until cooption is evident, then you bring the issue before the entire school community for a decision.

An example of this happened when the Skills Center through a state communication demanded that we administer and submit the reading scores of all our public aid recipients to them. Clearly this was another example of classifying and slotting people. Neither we, nor program participants, were ever able to receive a clear reason for this request of the Skill Center. We deduced it was probably to show the state was increasing reading levels for aid recipients and thereby qualifying for certain federal funds.

In any case we brought the problem to an all school meeting,and all members (including those not on public aid who would stand to lose all they'd worked for toward their high school diploma) decided to close the program before they'd concede to categorizing and classifying other members. That decision assured us, at least, that people were unwilling to simply 'make it' at others expense and that they saw the problem as a social-political one. A delegation of program participants met with a representative from the Skills Center and explained their position and what a 'rip-off' of aid recipients such a request represented. The discussion was heated and angry. Finally, they reached a compromise whereby our delegation said they would ask aid recipients to say what they thought their reading level was, thereby bypassing the test and trusting individual's sense of their own abilities. Even such a compromise did not go well with some; everyone reached consensus on the issue, however.

Many threats to the program's continuance happened frequently at the beginning of the program around discontinuance of funding issues. We had to charter a bus for Springfield where we intended to meet with Governor Walker to demand that our programs funds be continued. Most participants had to take off work thereby, losing a day's pay if they were paid hourly in order to make the trip. The red tape of getting to at least the Governor's assistant was frustrating for all of us. The eloquence of our participants demanding that a program such as ours which met real needs for poor people inspired many of us for the future struggle ahead of months of continued hassles around funding issues. We still remember the outrage and finally tears of Rosemary Sierra and Barbara Hampton as they sat facing the Governor's assistant at a long mahogany table in one of the highly formal rooms in the state capitol building.

We didn't lose our funding but not because of that action. In fact the bill we supported was defeated. Further, we didn't know if the Gov.'s assistant felt our pressure on the issue or if he was impressed. In a sense it didn't matter because we were impressed by each other, and renewed and inspirited again to struggle to keep a program we'd told each other mattered very much to people. We were to learn strategy and organizing techniques later. But in the beginning we had to understand what we were all willing to struggle for.

External And Internal Criticism Of Our Program

Critiques of our program seem to center on two issues. First, we are criticized for accepting funding from state/and or federal agencies when such support raises an alleged contradiction between our goal of transformation of the educational system, when we are in fact, in existence because of that very system. The implication is that we are thereby 'bought into' that system. Second, there is the question which confronts *Freire* about the action dimension of his process which also confronts us. The critique would run something like this—isn't our program simply a consciousness-raising process since the transformation of society demands a concrete action aimed directly at oppressive structures?

A response to the first question about public monies for radical education has been partially dealt with in an earlier section. The following is a somewhat fuller response. When we first initiated the program we were not funded and were doing organizing and preparation work on a volunteer basis. Two problems faced us in our idealism: one, how could we continue personally without funds and two, people interested in such a program wished an accredited high school diploma. Working for the transformation of society implies conscientization which most people who have appropriated the 'American Dream' of success haven't experienced. In order for people to be immersed in such a process we would have to respond to their immediate need and offer a high school diploma. Creating such a possibility demanded credentialed faculty to take responsibility for a full high school curriculum in order to meet the credit demands of North Central. All of this demanded some type of funding. Our conviction was/is that public monies belong to the people. We determined to accept these monies until the integrity of the program was threatened. Paolo Freire sums up our response to purist objections in a seminar held in Pontiac, Michigan in the summer of 1974—"in history you do what is possible." Further, if the question of cooption is pushed to its fullest logic one would do nothing.

The second question about action, is one we have struggled with continually. Initially we felt somewhat hysterical because there were people in the building (in classrooms!) instead of on the streets in public aid offices, health clinics, housing projects and factories. This anxiety for action misunderstood the dialectical relationship between reflection and action and over responded to action for the sake of action. Clearly we were being naive about our limits. Slowly we understood our action as a modest, albeit significant one. Modest, the way laying a foundation is modest. Our people worked all day, were involved in families and neighborhoods throughout the city. Their time and energy for actions were limited, and the practical reality of the fact that the program was only open in the evenings precluded many actions which were the logical follow-through to many of their political course experiences.

People did respond in action through marches and protests around struggles presented by visiting speakers from different organization, eg., Farmworkers, Fred Hampton Defense Committee, Alliance to End Repression, Casa and Angola Liberation Committee. Though they showed commitment to action, there was no single issue around which our entire group could organize.

It became clear to us that the common experience people shared was that they had been oppressed by an educational system. Their 'action' which our program provides the opportunity for is the possibility to reflect upon that experience, analyze the dominant systems education institution, and act to create a new possibility of their own. Intrinsic to that process, but not the direct result of it, is a critcal questioning of all institutions in America and specifically the dominant system's overarching structure which is capitalism.

A self criticism we struggle with is that it is primarily the members of the Governing Council who through their praxis transform educational systems. This would also be true of interest groups who come to the Council to make demands, the groups who initiated a Night Care program for participants' children, the group who began a Credit Union and Food Cooperative. The remaining members of the program, however, could be considered conscientized but not acting for transformation as yet.

One reason for these limits to a transformative praxis for all members is the fact that many participants can complete our program in from 10 to 20 weeks. We can't demand that people stay in the program longer when they should have received a diploma years ago. However, an attitude quetionaire we gave to people indicates that a significant change in consciousness which leads to deeper investment and action in the program takes place if people remain in the program 20 to 60 weeks.

Whenever our program has been threatened with closure because of funding or integrity issues, people have begun actions to keep the program alive. Any of the participants who went to the Skills Center offices, travelled to Springfield, went into the community to create a support base for our actions, have more fully realized through these actions their own ability to change structures, to create and defend their own educational effort.

The issue of faculty consciousness is still a problem for us. How can a new faculty member who may have the skills we need, be from the black community, know our area but not be conscientized themselves, be effective? They're not at first; they experience the process with participants and the participants teach them. It usually takes a new instructor, who is not familiarized with Freire, one or two semesters to understand the process.

What we wish to do in the interview process is discover the potential faculty members' understanding of how social change takes place; do they see change as helping people make it in the system or providing them with a chance to get a bigger peice of the pie? If potential faculty hold such assimilation goals (the American Dream of Success) we make clear the incompatible nature of their goals and our goals. This is not to say we have never hired faculty, who did not in some degree or another believe in the 'getting ahead' theory. This perspective is comparatively dominant among middle class blacks which a number of our instructors are. Having 'made it' themselves many black instructors wish to offer themselves and their achievement as an inspiration to others. All of this is perfectly understandable, but it fails to analyze the over all system of oppression most people in our program suffer; and such a consciousness fails to understand that most people won't 'make it' not because of any lack of talent or ability of theirs but because of the interstructing of race, class and sex bias.

Until last year all staff members at the beginning of each semester went on an arduous weekend seminar where we engaged our own conscientization process. Since that time challenges between faculty members about their politics and/or goals as members of our program have been relegated to faculty meetings and thereby minimized. Although many of us consider this lack of opportunity for dialogue a dilemma, the solution must come from the instructors' and facilitators' own organization.

A final question which confronts us is the question of effectiveness—does our program reach its goals? We have claimed that people in our program become more self-actualized, their alienation is diminished and fatalism overcome (personal tranformation) and that the program provides participants the choice to struggle to change their lives and the institutions which affect their lives (social transformation).

The way we measure our success is through the continual on-going evaluation process of the people in our program. Each course, each instructor, and each member through self and group evaluation is evaluated. The Governing Council evaluates each course and instructors. All program members evaluate the Governing Council. The Governing Council evaluates faculty and staff. Faculty evaluates the Administration and the Administration is evaluated by the Governing Council. Written evaluation (in addition to the group and individual process evaluation) on each course and instructors are reviewed by the Governing Council. All graduates write a written anonymous evaluation of the program and an essay statement on the program's effect on their lives. Although all of this written and formal evaluation is helpful to us, the on-going process evaluation is what inspires us and keeps us struggling. From all indications, based on participants criterion for success, we are reaching our goals. The criterion for success of our participants is that their lives have personally and socially changed, often dramatically, in positive and challenging directions.

The final evaluation of all efforts in our program is constructed by a simple question and answer which resounds our original dialogue with West side people before the program's inception. The question is this: for whom does the program exist? Whose interest does it serve? If the answer to that question is *us* , the people who make up the program, (and we are witnesses to the written, oral and story testimony that this is so) then the program is successful. The process of conscientization leads to such a question about ownership of the educational process. Unless that question is answered *by the people* affirmatively, nothing that's accomplished i.e., self actualized persons, everyone's values clarified, increased reading and math scores etc., really changes much of anything.

Finally, we are not suggesting that *every* member of our program is deeply conscientized, nor are we suggesting that people raise this question at every historical moment of their sojourn in the program. We are saying that for most people at some point in the process the question is raised in some form and is answered.

A more formal evaluation study will be conducted by Dr. Edgar Epps, a black educator of the University of Chicago who is interested in testing the theory, that our program facilitates achievement of self-autonomy and that feelings of powerlessness diminishes. Although this evaluation deals primarily with the personal tranformation dimension of the program, we feel it could be a useful evaluation. It is important to say, however, that it isn't this evaluation process, initated primarily as a justification of effectiveness to the Skills Center, which we trust. On the contrary, our trust is not in these scientific measures of effectiveness but in the people. We are of course taking a position, we aren't objective. We believe in this process because we see it working. We save our objectivity for critiques of us on our praxis—in such a dialogue our protectiveness, our investment, must be challenged by others who struggle for social tranformation as well as by ourselves.

It is not romanticism which causes us to return to the people's lives as the only measure of success in this process, it is realism. And so as this discussion on the effectiveness of the process ends we offer some words from the lives of one of a few hundred people who have graduated from our program.

Rosie Triplett supports 8 children, the second oldest of whom has cerebral palsey. "Until I came to the Adult Education program I never thought about my feelings or even that I was a person, not just a 'mother'. I didn't understand how much what I've experienced was understood and part of other black women's lives. My life is still changing, I take more risks, expect my children to risk more, be freer. I'm back at the Adult Education program to learn to be a group facilitator, I figure it's a way of paying back so other people can have the chance we've had. I want to do it. I've got this energy and ain't no way it's getting all used even by a full time job, some work in my housing project and 8 kids.".

1. Antoncich, Ricardo, S.J. notes from lecture, JSTC, Spring, 1975, p.2.
2. *Ibid.*, p. 11.

CHAPTER VI

The Liberation of Harijans in South Indian Villages

BY FELIX SUGIRTHARAJ

INTRODUCTION

This paper is addressed to those people who are speaking of a new language to redefine reality in which they live and who are seeking to critically analyze the socio-political situation which keeps the unjust structures unchanged. If they happen to read this paper, they will understand that it is not simply a theory, based on some optimistic ideology, but a true and live story which is being experienced by a group of committed young people in a typical oppressive rural context of India.

The message is that faith in humankind, faith in the future of man and of all people must be sustained. Let it be reviewed on the basis of what is taking place in the political life of our country today.

Who Am I? I am by birth an untouchable—a Harijan. I was born and raised in a small untouchable village in South India. My relatives are still uneducated, primitive, backward and extremely poor. I am thankful to the missionary movements which brought soup, soap and salvation to a large number of Harijans in Tamil Nadu. Since my grandparents became Christians, the missionaries agreed to put me in Christian mission schools and colleges for education. I am one of those few who have been richly benefitted by the Christian missionary activities in India.

I am also an ordained minister. I believe in Jesus Christ and His salvation. The Bible teaches that liberation of people involves historical projection for the creation of a new man and a new social solidarity. In relation to my faith, liberation is freedom *from* bondage and freedom for love and fellowship with God and all men. Therefore, hatred, misery, suffering, poverty, hopelessness and discrimination are not any longer laid at the door of fate or superstititon, but on men who are responsible for the society. My stance is not to physically convert others into Christianity or to claim that Christianity is the only religion that has the answer to all the Harijan problems, but to witness to the righteousness and justice of God in the liberation of my fellow-men at whatever risk may be involved. From 1965-1973, I worked among slum dwellers in the city of Madras. With the co-operation of other social welfare organizations, a team of us tried new techniques, including community organization, to build up a strong, powerful force to tackle social issues. But we discovered that the slum dwellers have deep seated village characteristics which make them believe that ultimately they will go back to their villages and live a life of security and sufficiency.

It was then, I decided to go back to the rural areas from where I came some years ago. I was also convinced that our program failed because we treated the urban poor as objects of charity and never taught them to identify their own problems and participate in democratic change. About 75% of our population is rural. They bear the responsibilities of producing food. The worsening economic trends, combined with population explosion force them to give up their own rights and responsibilities in the hands of a few, powerful elite and lose all hopes and visions of a new India. I engaged in research to discover the actual problems of the rural sector and came up with the following conclusions.

Causes for Underdevelopment in Rural India (1) The problem of the rural poor is viewed as social rather than economic, as institutional rather than technological. These two do not have to be neglected, but these factors have to be viewed within the context of the total social situation. The problem of landlessness threatens the lives of millions of rural people. More than 60% are landless, 30% are petty farmers or tenants, and the rest are rich, caste landlords who own enormous amounts of land. Any attempt to remedy the situation by means of land reform has not been very successful since legislation concerning land reforms has been enacted by the very same people against whom it is supposed to militate. The legislation is therefore not much less than a gimmick of the powerful elite, as it intends to keep the untouchable agricultural labor under bondage to a moneyed caste for many years to come. The poverty of the petty farmer and the laborer is reflected in the low levels of essential elements of human development such as educational proportion, food intake, aspiration for a better life etc. The landless laborer has only one desire—to survive. By force of circumstances, he has been used to a life below or just within the level of subsistence. To maintain the allegiance of rural poor, the powerful elite has kept them poor and dependent and extended material support which has to be regained in one way or another. The paternalistic spirit on the part of the powerful elite towards their dependents, who in turn offer their political allegiance without meaningful participation, has kept the dependents economically poor, and socially immobile. The vertical relationship of the masses to power groups in the country explains the phenomenon of castism, factionalism, communalism etc., fragmenting the country into economic and political groups.

In the name of rural improvement, government and private agencies have been organized to serve the rural sector. Despite the tremendous efforts made, these agencies, instead of militating against the social structures, the main source of insecurity, operate within and maintain and strengthen the same social structure. Their efforts suffer from the following inefficiencies: (a) the failure to politicalize the villagers due to non-recognition of formal and non-formal leaders in the identification of the felt needs; (b) the extreme red tapism experienced by rural people dealing with government agencies; (c) wastage of funds due to a network of graft and corruption existing at all levels of society; (d) overlapping of function in government and private agencies; (e) isolation of projects doomed to failure due to lack of planning at the local and national level and allocation of funds; (f) failure to translate the findings of research both in socio-cultural field and technology in a language that rural people and agricultural workers understand.

Rural people left to themselves do not possess the self-confidence to organize themselves so as to pressure the government to satisfy their basic needs. Nor do they realize that the solution to the problem lies first of all in understanding that the social situation is related to their tragic economic condition. This new understanding requires further an awareness of other factors, including the following: poor infra-structure, lack of credit facilities, lack of effective marketing, under utilization of labor, population explosion and absence of knowledge of modern technology.

(2) The changing of the ideology of the ruling party—the Congress Party—from time to time is the other reason for rural under-development. Gandhi and Nehru had the vision of treating the people as subjects and not as objects of history. People have been objects of exploitation in the past. Both Gandhi and Nehru wanted to stimulate the political process which would awaken them to their conditions of independence and make them ready to struggle consciously for their rights, not merely of bread and welfare, but of freedom and social justice. Gandhi made the people's self-rule in village societies the basis of his Swanaj (movement). Nehru, on the other hand, made room for people to think for themselves and organize themselves in parties for self-awakening and participation. But today their legacy has been negated by many changes even in the parliamentary structure with legal justification.

(3) The third problem is the *evils of the caste system* which has rendered our society undemocratic and made equality a myth to 20 million untouchables. Unless Hindu reformers come forward to do away with the doctrines of castism in Hindu religion, there is very little chance for the untouchables to claim equal rights and privileges in Indian society. Every Hindu believes that he belongs to a caste and has to live according to his status in society. His wealth, property, employment, social status are all regarded as a gift from God which is predestined according to the merits of dharma (good deeds) in the previous birth.

The untouchables do not belong to the Hindu caste structure. They have been segregated from the caste villages and allowed to live in outcaste villages at a distance of at least one mile bearing the name Cheri (a slum of untouchables). They have been exploited physically, socially, economically and politically for centuries. Still they are not allowed to walk with shoes on the streets of the caste villages and are taught to stand half-naked before a caste man as a mark of respect to their masters—the landlords. If a high caste man touches an untouchable, he has to perform a rite of purification to get rid of uncleanliness. Though Article 17 of the Constitution proclaims that untouchability is abolished and its practice in any form is forbidden, still discrimination is continued all over India. Should they, who are the cream of agricultural labor, be allowed to live and die as unwanted citizens of Indian society?

PART I

A. FROM CITY TO VILLAGE

In June 1974, I left the city of Madras and went over to live in a small untouchable village on the south eastern coast of India. I did have contacts with some of the villagers even before I went there. I organized a summer camp for a group of trainees in community organization during 1973 and did an extensive survey to analyze the socio-economic conditions of the rural poor. The trainees used a sample of one thousand families of untouchable and caste spread over an area of 20 square miles. The sample provided ample evidences that the untouchables, though, were more in number, have been exploited constantly by the powerful landlords, each possessing a hundred to two hundred acres of wet land. The stories of injustice told by the untouchables revealed the fact that they have been living in fear and misery.

After renting a hut to live in, I recruited young, educated college graduates who are untouchables by birth. Some of the young people who worked in Madras and got disgusted with city life were also interested in working with me as a team. After recruiting 15 people, we planned and organized a study camp for ourselves in a lonely travellers lodge near a sea shore—close to my village. We remained there for a month to study and assess the cultural, social and political situation of India after independence with future perspective of Harijan (untouchable) development in mind. We spent half of our time visiting a few untouchable villages and surveying the oppressive situation. We held discussion and interviews with a few untouchable leaders who were more anxious and enthusiastic to stand against powerlessness. A few speakers such as agricultural experts, professors of sociology and political science were invited to speak to us on various subjects related to rural development and progress. A few case studies which revealed the nature of the social injustices were analyzed. We spent considerable amount of time in prayer, Bible study and devotions to discover the relevancy of the Gospel in the liberation of the untouchables.

We studied a few models and theories used for liberation in the Third World and picked up the methodology used by Paulo Freire, the Brazilian educationist. Further, Gandhi's mass participation method through non-violence was found relevant to the rural situation.

An Adult Education Process For Untouchables. After careful thought and preparation, we wrote our aims and objectives of education for liberation combing the educational theories of Gandhi and Paulo Freire. We decided to use adult education as the first step to mobilize the untouchables. It is important to point out the significance of Gandhi's and Freire's models for authentic education which we accepted our way towards liberation.

B. Gandhi's Approach To Education For Liberation

To Gandhi liberation meant three things: 1) Liberation of the individual in the struggle within. 2) Liberation of the country from the colonial rule. 3) Liberation from external aggression.

All of Gandhi's programs were contemplated to cover a comprehensive canvas. One of the most significant synthesis was an effort to bring together the program of purification of the self with the social revolution. His concept of education covered both education within school system as well as education within the society as a whole. Outside the school system, his whole program of Satyagraha (mass participation for liberation through non-violent means) was based on mass education for social change. It had both positive and negative aspects. The negative program was to resist evil through non-violence using the following elements: a) Being aware of the injustice in the situation. b) Refusing to comply with the process on the structure perpetrating injustice. c) Readiness to suffer in the process of resistance. d) Organization of the resistance through a movement. The positive program was to create the condition for just society. It includes: a) Economic self dependence. b) Unity among different organizations within. c) Organizations of sections such as labor, students, women, etc. All these programs would be implemented through a struggle. It includes: a) A deep sense of respect for the people. b) Working with them in their own language. c) Living and identifying with them in every respect. d) Sacrificing all comforts and becoming servants. e) Involving people to make decisions in all activities. The self purification aspect includes observance of truth, non-violence and non-possession. It is not an individual act. It is practised in the community by listening to others, by silence and contemplation, through singing, fasting and meditating.

C. Paulo Freire's Approach To Education For Liberation

Freire is an important critic of the present educational system. He developed his method for teaching illiterates while he was a professor of history and education in the University of Recife in Brazil. Educational enterprise, observes Freire, is always a device for the imposition of the ideas of the ruling class on the masses. It is the pedagogy of oppression. Instead of communication, the teacher issues communiques, and makes deposits, which students patiently receive, memorize and repeat. This is a banking system of education. But Freire proposes a "problem posing" education whose objectives will be personal and social liberation. In this system, the students are no longer "docile listeners," but critical co-investigators in dialogue with the teacher. He demonstrated this methodology in the adult education programs in Brazil and Chile with great success. In those programs people participated in one another's education and made it a common pursuit on the basis of critical thinking and dialogue—the core of problem solving education.

According to Freire, education is a revolutionary stance for the liberation of the oppressed. Through union between reflection and action, it is possible to raise the consciousness of the people. It is a process in which men, not as recipients but as knowing subjects, achieve a deepening awareness both of the socio-cultural reality which shapes their lives and of their capacity to transform that reality. This occurs not by intellectual effort, but by praxis. This process is called by Freire as "conscientization." Speaking about cultural action and cultural revolution through conscientization, Freire criticises the Right for not being utopic. According to him, the Right denounce reality without knowing reality, proclaim a new reality without a draft project, make new myths out of the denunciation, and renounce communion with the people. But the revolutionary utopia tends to be dynamic rather than static; tends to life rather than death; to the future as a challenge to man's creativity rather than a repetition of the present; to love as liberation of subjects rather than as pathological possessiveness; to dialogue rather than muteness; to harmony rather than gregariousness; to praxis than to law and order. Revolutionaries must prove their respect for the people, their feeling and confidence in them, not as a strategy, but as an implicit requirement. The role is to help people move from the levels of naive-transitive consciousness to the level of critical consciousness. Originating in the praxis of both the leadership and the rank and file, every revolutionary project is basically "cultural action" in the process of becoming a "cultural revolution." Communion with the people in day to day's affairs is one of the fundamental characteristics of cultural action for freedom.

D. The Aims And Objectives Of Our Movement

Man has to be freed from the powers that oppress, cultures that keep him numb, beliefs and cults that keep him silent and primitive, structures that curtail his freedom and dignity. Therefore, liberation should begin with a dialogue that interests people. Since 90% of the untouchables are illiterates, they are more attracted to an adult education program that fascinates them than any other form of cultural action. The adult education program is only a starting point. Sooner or later other cultural actions which are suggested by the people will be carried on. The ultimate aim is to bring a reality transformation in each learner and participant. The whole program is geared towards total formation of the human person for his own welfare as well as the welfare of others around him. It must contribute to the building up of a humane, just society around the community. Reverence for all life, brotherhood of his fellowmen and patience and endurance during trouble should become the foundation of this process. "Education is not what a person learns, but what he becomes." Teaching to read and write is only a secondary aim. The primary purpose is to raise the level of consciousness through effective vehicles of communication and sensitize people for mass action, leading to social and political change. We do not believe in an ideology of paternalism, social control and non-reciprocity between experts and helpees. On the other hand, we are ideologically committed to equality, to the abolition of priveleges, and to a non-elitist form of leadership.

E. Goals And Methods

1. Cultural action through adult education, dramas, dance, story telling etc., to illiterate men, women and children will lead people ultimately to critical consciousness and social transformation.
2. Training of village leaders (formal and informal) young adults and educated youth will result in politicalization and mass action on issues which are pertinent to the community.
3. Living together, working together, suffering together and sharing together will build the character and create confidence and trust in each other.
4. Forming and organizing inter-village committees on community organization lines, with special emphasis for economic and social reforms, will build up a powerful Untouchable Labor Organization for effective political action.

F. Formation Of The Group

After reaching a consensus that the area, where the camp was held needed our service very badly, we decided to stay in that area for a period of three months to find out whether we could build up solidarity with the people and work hand in hand with them, for liberation. Out of fifteen, only seven took the challenge seriously and decided to stay. We named ourselves as Action for Cultural, Social and Political Change and dedicated ourselves to serve those people. These young graduates, who happen to be untouchables, made four vows before they started their work. (1) They would work in the movement for a period of three years and accept hardships and financial strains as a challenge. (2) They would not seek comfort, but accept simple way of village life and try to live in the untouchable villages and lead a humble life. (3) They would lead a life of Christian discipline based on prayer, scripture reading and meditation and promise to use non-violence as an effective weapon in any circumstance. (4) They would not exploit or control the villagers, but would accept the role of a servant to the villagers.

Part II

A Choice Of The Area

Since it was agreed to work in the same area where the camp was held, the seven of us decided to do a thorough sociological survey to discover the weaknesses and potentialities of the villages. An area of 25 square miles with 48 villages was taken as a boundary for the first stage of work.

B. Study Of The Area

Each member of the group would take five villages for survey. He would travel extensively around these villages, observing and learning the whole characteristics of the village life and understand the concrete life situations. He would talk to the villagers and record cases of injustices, exploitation, discrimination and victimization. He would use his own discretion to study carefully the economic backwardness, conflicting situations, educational standards, religious beliefs and myths, leadership trends etc., and assess the potentialities and the victimised condition of a village. If the villagers are very receptive and offer a hint to stay, he would hold a mass meeting at the street corner and clear all the doubts and suspicions of the people. He would also explain the aims and objectives of our group and wait for the reaction and responses. If people agree whole-heartedly to allow him to stay, he would do so.

Weekly staff meetings were held for feed back and selection of the villages. After strenuous survey work for a month, nine key villages were chosen. These villages would be the residence of each main graduate animater. Data collection through the help of questionaires to assess economic situation, the causes of poverty, the percentage of illiteracy, social and political condition etc., were all done systematically in the initial stages to determine whether we were doing the right thing or not. It has been very helpful for us to have conducted the survey by ourselves. If we had sought the help of a professional research assistant, many revealing facts would have remained unknown.

C. Description Of The Area

This is situated at the 65th mile of the city of Madras on the south eastern coast of India. This is the most backward area in the whole district (country) of Tamil Nadu (state) with the largest number of Harijans. Ninety six percent of the Harijans are landless laborers who depend upon the rich caste landowners for employment and survival. Most of the villages are linked by mud roads and are reached by bicycles. These 48 villages come under one block (The Government Office for Rural Community Development). The elected president is ably supported by 42 caste representatives who are elected by the village councils. Though the majority are Harijans, only six representatives are on the governing body of the block. They are the staunch supporters of the caste landlords. Geographically, though a village is called by only one name, there will be a distance of one or two miles dividing the caste and the untouchable village. The untouchable village is always mentioned as *Cheri* (a slum). The untouchable villagers usually address themselves as "Cheri" people. Welfare facilities to each village will be in terms of two separate units—caste and outcaste colonies. Schools, wells for drinking, burial grounds, temples are always treated as separate entities.

D. Organization Of The Group

The seven Harijan college graduates are designated as *Main Animaters.* An animater is one who inspires, excites and encourages people to act for good. He is not a social worker or a community organizer. He is not a leader, but an enabler, playing a humble role of servant with selflessness and sensitiveness. He is not an outsider, but one who is available at all times for the service of the village community. He animates and enables people to respond creatively in all circumstances. We have been working in this area since August 1974. There is no director or co-ordinator. Each has equal power and control over others. We live in key villages and cover at least six to seven villages each. Our main task is to initiate cultural action programs such as adult and children's literacy classes, cultural dramas, sports, etc., conduct training programs for village animaters and village leaders and women, etc., with the consent and the co-operation of the villagers. We also help people to write petitions and letters, accompany villagers when they are meeting government officers, defend and support villagers when they are in trouble and enable villagers to participate actively in village and inter-village meetings and sew the seeds of mass labor organization.

The Village Animaters are young and energetic men and women who have a fair standard of education. They are chosen from the local villages by the people as well as by us (main animaters). The criteria for selection is based on their critical sense, leadership qualities and various other capacities. They work closely with the main animaters and two village leaders. They represent a progressive radical group who are interested in political change. Each main animater will be assisted by three or four village animaters.

The Village Leaders are voluntary workers. They are the people who understand the significance of the movement before they let us into the villages. By contract, they are responsible in arranging all programs, dramas and meetings and attend all sessions where strategies to tackle problems are discussed. They have great confidence in us as we do trust them. They are the backbone of our movement. They are mostly between 30 to 50 years of age. They are supposed to carry out the liberation struggle even after our departure. They are also the future pillars who have to build a solid, powerful, well knit Harijan Union. As of now, we have about 50 strong leaders who have undergone disciplined leadership training by us.

Part III

A. Cultural Action For Conscientization

1. Literacy Program For The Whole Village

Once the main animater settles in a village, he gets to know all the people by talking to them at all times. To become fully aware of the richness of each village culture, he collects about 200 to 300 words which are frequently used by the people day after day. Through these common words, he is able to understand the slangs, jargons and the traditional symbols of each village. This is called a "vocabulary analysis."

Every evening he is supposed to write his daily diary. Each main animater will write down all of what he hears and understands, and his diary is maintained as a record book in each village. The diary will contain matters such as the past and present history of the village, the facts of injustices, the traditional values, cultural differences, common problems, political awareness etc. The main animater will select at least 25 key words out of 300 on the basis of their historical significance and the richness of phonetic and semantic sounds. Each key village will have a population of six hundred to eight hundred people.

a. *Vocabulary analysis* consists of words such as boy, girl, lamp, hut, land, tree, water, well, work, school, teacher, radio, cattle, sheep, garden, rice, vegetables, cart, police, landlord, wages, cheri, gruel, pickle, devil, goddess, small pox, cholera, cycle, etc.

b. *The Key Words* (First Stage) which are chosen from the analysis are: hut, land, water, well work, school, rice, wages, landlord, cheri, devil, etc. For example, tree or radio has no social or cultural significance. Tree gives shade or used for firewood. Radio is not a common thing in a Harijan village. But key words such as hut, water, rice, wage, etc., have a lot of economic, social, cultural and religious significance.

A hut is something where a Harijan lives. It is small, not strong, built only with mud and coconut leaves, not airy or spacious. The Harijan is forced to live all his life in a hut whereas the landlord, in a caste village, lives in a terraced house with all amenities. The word hut is indirectly connected with land problem, village underdevelopment, financial problems, health problems, and many other social problems related to local and national levels. Key words will be recorded in a separate note book and a syllabus will be written on each word. The word will be codified and de-codified. Codification means to inter-link words of the same sound for literacy value, e.g. hut, put, but, etc. Codification also anaylzes and finds out the richness of the word in the historical, social, cultural and religious setting as illustrated below.

H	U	T
B	U	T
P	U	T

(An illustration example)

De-codify: words related to hut, e.g. land, slum, inadequate space, housing, injustice, inequality, etc.

Illustrate through a drawing how a hut looks like compared to the big house of the landlord. The landlord's cattle shed is bigger than the hut of a Harijan. Explain how a model village will be built. Raise initial questions such as who provides land for free cost housing? How much it costs? Who can provide money? What is the responsibility of the village council? What do the local and national government do for poor people's housing? Why does a Harijan suffer with poor housing? Who has to be blamed? What can be done to repair bad housing? What can be the long range plan? Who can approve the plan? What will be the reaction of the caste people? Dialogue and discussion will bring new insights and critical awareness among the villagers.

Teaching people how to write: demonstrate on the black board how to write. Word learning (literacy) comes at the very end after a long discussion regarding the hut problem.

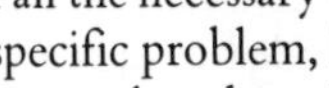

(An illustration example)

If the above illustration, for instance, is known to the people, any word in our language can be taught. For example, hut in our language is written as: 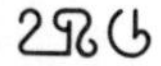
Note the similarity to the above illustration example. These lines (illustration example) are called vertical lines, horizontal lines, half circles, full circles and hook lines.

After a thorough preparation of all the necessary things, the main animater takes the class. If he has any doubt about a specific problem, he is not supposed to take the class unless his doubts are clarified. For every *class,* the animater has to decide on time, place, people and subjects. Usually the time is limited to one to one and a half hour. This is usually between 8:00-9:00 p.m. every evening except Sundays. The place will be the street corner where light facilities are available. Learners consist of the whole village people—men, women and children. Blackboards, pencils, charts, pictures, etc., are the only available visual aids. People are taught to write on the sand with their fingers in unison.

Dialogue and discussion can continue the next morning or the following night until people understand the problematizing process. Sometimes it may take two weeks to end up discussing each important word. All dialogue and discussions will be held on the basis of reflection—action process. Both men and women will be allowed to speak during the classes. The animater's role is to initiate the discussion and keep it going. He should see that one person does not dominate. He will carefully observe the depth of the discussion and discover potential leaders. He will raise relevant questions to make them think and come out of their apathy and despair. Vital issues will be presented again in the leadership meetings for discussion. The animater should show the importance of the issue and create an atmosphere in which everyone begins to talk about it the next day. Only then conscientization is possible. The issues should become realistic and lively. They must penetrate their hearts and disturb them.

c. *Action.* If a suitable decision is made to re-vitalize the issue, techniques such as role plays, etc., will be used before concrete action takes place. The same issue will be magnified in other villages to win the support and sympathy of the villagers and to co-operate in a joint venture. The success of the issue depends on the problematization of the key word. Non-violent and peaceful agitative methods will be followed if mass protest has to be planned. It might take six months to cover all the twenty five key words. An evaluation was conducted after six months to assess the effectiveness of each program and the reaction of the people to them. As a sample, fifty men and fifty women plus fifty non-school going children were interviewed in five different villages where programs were organized regularly.

d. *The results* of the literacy program were encouraging. About 75% of the adults (men and women) said that they learnt more about their oppressive condition than before. Most of them said that they never learnt that much before. Twenty five percent wanted to learn to read and write. Fifty percent were happy because they were able to sign their names now. Women felt that they could have participated more if they had separate classes. School going children who attended the classes voluntarily proclaimed that they were able to learn more in our classes than in the school. The non-school going children did not appreciate the program very much. Everyone preferred the classes conducted in the street corner of different streets. The villagers agreed to buy a petromax light with their own money.

From this assessment, we were able to accept the fact that men are capable of acting and perceiving, Of knowing and recreating. We observed certain amount of critical consciousness among people regarding the attitude of the oppressive reality around them

e. *Second Stage.* Another 25 words were picked up from the 300 word vocabulary analysis, and a new syllabus was prepared for the next six months. Emphasis was given to school dropouts and non-school going children. It was felt that they should not be separated but learn along with the adults and get to know about their pathetic condition from now on. It was decided to start the classes a little earlier and conduct creativity games and word building skits for the children. The program was extended to seven more villages and the village animaters were given the responsibilities to take classes in some villages.

2. *Cultural Dramas for Harijan Villages*

a. *Purpose:* 1) To create a sense of unity between one village and another. 2) To bring the villagers together in a common place once a week or twice a month to provide political education on common issues. 3) To caricature oppressors and exploiters through true stories and events and curb alienation and lethargy. 4) To provide entertainment and recreation which has no place in their lives. 5) To train young villagers how to be creative—to encourage innovation instead of merely carrying out orders blindly. 6) To help the people to reject cultural myths which confuse their awareness and make them ambiguous beings.

b. *Myths* such as "all are equal," "all belong to one village," "if we work hard we can become landlords," "do charity and increase God's blessings," "tea shop is meant for all," "make sacrifice to appease God," etc., were often remarked during dramas to show that myths do not liberate Harijans, but de-humanize them.

c. *Taboos* such as, after dark don't go out alone, diseases are due to the anger of the goddess, education will make a man unemployed, women are meant to cook the food, witch-craft is better than modern medicine, etc., are repeated and enacted as untruthful and superstitious.

d. *Different stages of drama:* 1) Totally neutral, e.g., comics, jokes and funny stories from scriptures and fairy tales emphasizing one moral.
2) Problems in which minority of the people are included—beggars, hoodlums, drunkards, bootleggers etc. 3) Problems in which majority is involved—illiteracy, diseases, wage problems, housing etc. 4) Key people will be involved, e.g. political leaders, villager leaders, unjust landlords, exploiting shop keepers etc. 5) Slogans and action programs—How to demand more wages? How to tackle the landlord and a money lender? How to contest and win the election, etc?

e. *Methodology For Drama.* Oppressive situations will be enacted to prove the cause of injustice and show the way of overcoming it. Stories and scripts are based on social and political themes only. The main animaters, village animaters and the village leaders choose and discuss the themes and scripts in advance at leadership meetings and hold rehearsals. The whole drama with actors will be rehearsed a number of times so that each actor would know what to say and how to act. Music is provided by the villagers. The Harijans are good drummers. So far drums are beaten only during funerals. Since the drum is made out of cow skin, the caste people hate drumming. During dramatization the Harijans are encouraged to use the drums, thus magnifying aspects of their culture. Each village is responsible for erecting the stage, arranging for the lights etc., in a common open space where people sit on the ground and watch the drama. Though dramas during festivals will go on throughout the night, we realize that villagers have no energy to keep awake throughout the night and watch the drama. Our dramas are short and crisp, touching and sensitizing the people. At least four villages participate in each drama.

Since drama is an effective mass communication media, we once again use the dialogue method for effective communication. Since the stage is only a tool above the ground, the actors will have access to walk through the crowd when necessary. In any scene, the actors will raise questions and try to find answers from the audience. For instance, someone acts like a shopkeeper, he will ask the crowd, "Is it true that I sell goods for more money? This is what people think? I hope you don't think so! Do you?" The audience will shout at him and blame him for all his evil vices and exploitation. A woman who has mortgaged her only earring will get up spontaneously and accuse the actor as though he is the actual shopkeeper. When another actor emphasizes the idea of fair price shop, he will speak about the pros and cons and the co-operation needed to form such a thing. If anybody has a doubt, he can stand and talk or raise questions. During the drama, if the whole audience agrees on a development program suitable to the village, the planning will take place the next day. Sometimes, committee members for various development programs and action groups will be elected during the dramas.

f. *Results.* Within six months, 15 dramas were staged. We generally do not enact dramas in the villages where our programs are not intensified. Again, the people have to decide the time, place and subject for the next drama in their village action committees. Though dramas politicized people for mass action, they caused many clashes and controversies with the caste people. Conflicts emerged many a time, but were solved amiably with the timely intervention of the leaders and police. We keep the police informed of our activities well in advance and incite them occasionally to witness what is going on.

So far the religious and cultural dramas, organized by the landlords and caste people once or twice a year, were based on myths, without exposing reality to the people. They never oriented the people to the unveiling of reality, since this would mean denunciation or accepting people's decisions. But now, critical consciousness is brought about not through an intellectual effort, but simply through proxy, through a genuine dialogue which reflects in an authentic union between reflection and action. True cultural action, according to Paulo Freire, can be satisfied neither with the mystifications of ideology nor with a simple moral denunciation of myths and errors but must undertake a rational and rigorous action, based on the truth of reality.

Today, the real stories and plots are all chosen by the villagers and put into a real drama which is focussed on a liberated village life. Traditionally, drama actors who staged plays during Hindu festivals were all high caste professionals. But our young Harijan men have broken that tradition and proved that they are much better actors with more creativity, talent and common sense. It is true that drama breaks away the culture of silence and infuses the spirit of cultural action.

3. *Leadership Training And Action Committees*

a. Aims. As the mass education programs are intensified, the animaters look out for people, both young and old with energy, intelligence and experience to train and form action committees in villages. Like the other programs leadership training also constitutes an interacting totality of objectives, methods and procedures. It is in these groups, we prove our respect for the people, and insist upon working together with a lot of sharing and learning from each other. We believe that commitment to the people comes not only through mass programs but through working in nuclear groups. Once again, problematization will be the goal of this training. It means both asking questions and calling into questions various injust situations which are un-noticed though they exist side by side oppressing people. Problematization does not come easily to silent, passive masses. The key role of the animater is to challenge both the people and the reality to be studied. Once again the theory is based on dialogue, that is the examination of each situation by conscious people who stand in a subject-to-subject relationship to one another.

b. *Practice.* We meet these leaders twice a week in our own huts. We do not arrange the training in open air. The training and discussion involve certain amount of concentration and discipline. The subject and the syllabus for the training and meetings are chosen by the people after a throrough examination of the importance of each topic. Meetings are held usually after 9 p.m. The subjects that have been dealt with so far are: the importance of the rural population in the Indian context, the difference between development and liberation, how to organize and conduct meetings, how to analyze issues—crucial and non-crucial, how to form inter-village committees, national issues on castism, the history of Harijan culture, welfare programs of the government to Harijans, Gandhi and his ideology, how non-violence can be structured in villages, the state legislation towards landless and agricultural employees, the Twenty Point program of the government, how to tackle the government officials, the privileges and rights of village citizens, the meaning of local self government.

Apart from regular group meetings and training, an inter-village meeting is called for once a month with four or five village action committee representatives. Important economic, social and political issues will be discussed and decisions will be made for mass action. The leaders serve as a link between people and the leadership meetings. The next day, the leaders will explain the resolutions of the inter-village meetings and enlist the support of the whole village. This is done during literacy on drama programs.

c. *Issues—How Are They Tackled?* Example: the Twenty Point program of the government specifically supports any attempt made by the Harijans to get free house plots. In a particular untouchable village, the residents have been squatting on the land of the caste man for the past 20 years without owning the plots. The landlord says he is very paternalistic. But nobody realized how he has benefitted. As long as the people stay there, he can depend on unconditional cheap labor to work in his fields which are vast and very productive. The villagers have come across a piece of land that has been laying waste for the past 30 years. It belongs to the state. Therefore, they plan carefully to approach the concerned officers of the government to donate house plots in the vacant land. This whole process involves calling for local village governing body, resolution, the ways and means of approaching, the rules and regulation, the unity and interest of the villagers, the co-operation of the caste people to a certain extent, petition writing, model plan, organization for action etc. The success and the struggle is shared with joy and sorrow by the whole village. But amidst all this, we can see the emergence of the popular consciousness, which is in the process of applying pressure on the power structure for the new age of transformation. For the first time in history, the powerful caste landlords have found themselves unmasked by the so called silent masses. Controversies and conflicts arise one after another while the tension between the masses become anxious to be set free, and the powerful become anxious to maintain the status quo is seen in climax. But in this transitional situation, the closed caste power structures slowly yield to a dynamism in a few dimenstions of social life.

PART IV

A. WHAT IS NEXT?

The transitional phase has generated a new style of social and political life in the populist leadership. Though the life-style of the oppressive caste society goes through slight changes, the Harijans are not able to raise their voices and speak on their own behalf. The power of the populist leadership manipulates its own community, but it does not affect the caste people very much.

At this stage, we are wondering whether the leaders will play a responsible and creative role in the formation of a legal structure which can make them independent, powerful and demanding according to the law. As per the provision granted by the Federal Government, a landless agricultural labor union could have been formed if the people desired. But the emergency law prohibits the formation and all activities of labor organization in the country. Under these cirucumstances, it is interesting to watch the results of this movement stage by stage. People are nor realizing that they should not follow directional signals and lose their thinking and creative capacity. Imagination and critical sense are converting their fatalistic beliefs that Harijans are created to grope in the dark and end up in hell. It is our belief that they will continue to struggle from their governed, subjugated, invaded community into a society of human character built on freedom, justice and equality.

Conclusion

Our movement is not a blue print to be copied or tried some where else. Our concern for the people is so central that it rules out any policy which does not become truly theirs. Those who are oppressed do not enjoy the freedom to fail, the luxury of experimenting. But somewhere we see the speck of hope — the hope of liberation, freedom and power, emerging out of a condemned, helpless, oppressed community. Our utopianism is no idealistic dream spun out of a mind ideologically. It grows out of our practical involvement with the oppressed in a process of both becoming conscientized. Our Christian faith invites us to a new Exodus. We are moving forward, forever dying, forever being reborn. We accept an existence which is in dramatic tension between the past and the future, staying and going, being and not being. Our guiding motto has been and will be "Expect Great Things From God: Attempt Great Things For God."

CHAPTER VII

A New Public Ministry: The Christian Urgent Action Network for El Salvador

BY STEVEN F. DURHAM

I. MIGUEL

Following worship services on Sunday, October 28, 1984, the pastor of San Salvador's Emmanuel Baptist Church—the Rev. Miguel Tomas Castro Garcia, 32—left the church with one of his daughters to drive two parishioners home. A short distance away a blue Chevy van pulled in front of Miguel's car and blocked its progress, while a white Toyota pulled in behind and blocked any retreat.

Three men in civilian clothes, armed with machine guns, got out of the van, forced the occupants of Miguel's car to the sidewalk, and demanded to see identification. When Miguel gave his name his assailants threw a plastic hood over his head, causing him difficulty in breathing, and beat him in the stomach with the butts of their weapons. He then was shoved into the van and driven away. One of the parishioners had the presence of mind to write down the van's license number.

Miguel was taken to an underground cell at the headquarters of El Salvador's National Police in downtown San Salvador. There he was blindfolded and forced to remain standing for the duration of what proved to be a 52 hour interrogation. His interrogators worked in rotating shifts of eight. Miguel, his family and members of the church continually were threatened with death if he failed to cooperate in providing answers. As if to prove their point, his interrogators at regular intervals put a gun to Miguel's head and pulled the trigger. At one point late in the interrogation he was driven in perhaps the original blue van back to his church where he was made to identify persons entering and leaving the building. One of these proved to be his mother; but, in line with the evasive answers given about the identity of others, Miguel responded by saying she was just an old woman who came to Emmanuel to worship on occasion, about whom he knew little else.

Today, from exile in Mexico where he lives with his family, Miguel says without qualification that the reason he is alive is because of the intervention of a North American church-based telegram network. This network, through the agency of over 1000 telegrams and phone calls to appropriate government offices in San Salvador (including the U.S. Embassy), created sufficient publicity to prevent Miguel's "disappearance" into the penal system—a "disappearance" which most likely would have ended in his torture and death. Instead, Miguel was forced to sign a document indicating he was a "guerrilla" and that his church's extensive refugee relief work actually supported the "guerrillas"; but he came away relatively unharmed and was sent into exile. (Baptist leaders in El Salvador later were summoned to the office of the Director of the National Police. There they were told, in a bizarre meeting complete with prayer and Bible reading initiated by the Director, that in fact there were insufficient grounds for sustaining any charges against Miguel.)

The intervening North American network—the Christian Urgent Action Network for El Salvador (CUANES, pronounced 'KWANace")—forms the subject of this paper. In eleven months of operations CUANES has been involoved in the successful release of six church workers. It also publicized demands for an inquiry into the torture/murder of a Lutheran pastor, a campaign leading ultimately to two arrests. Based on these results it safely can be said CUANES not only "works", but also provides a strong model for a new kind of public ministry. These assertions will be evaluated in the course of this paper.

II. Background

Sources

CUANES is a church-based urgent action network designed to respond to the abduction of church workers in El Salvador by publicizing the abduction. Such publicity serves to increase the chances of the abducted person's survival and avoidance of torture. The network operates under the auspices of the Presbytery of Chicago (regional governing body for churches in the Presbyterian Church [U.S.A.] in metropolitan Chicago). The writer serves as U.S. Coordinator for CUANES.

The model for the network comes from two sources. One obvious source is Amnesty International (AI), the pioneer in creating publicity about abducted persons in order to prevent possible torture and death. AI in fact was considered as a possible organizer of what came to be CUANES, but declined the request for reasons to be discussed below.

The second model was an actual case in El Salvador. In early 1983 a Lutheran medical missions worker, Dr. Angel Ibarra, was abducted by security forces. North American Lutherans responded by creating an *ad hoc* network, including European churches, which sustained pressure on the Salvadoran government in the form of unrelenting publicity. Six months later Dr. Ibarra was released. He now lives in exile in Canada. He had been tortured; but the case was considered a "success" simply because Dr. Ibarra survived.

Decisions

Based primarily on Dr. Ibarra's case Salvadoran church leaders in late 1983 approached a number of North American groups, including AI, about the possibility of forming a permanent church-based telegram network. The Presbytery of Chicago was one of those approached by Salvadoran church leadership which worked primarily through an intermediary.

AI declined to organize the network in part because of the way their own urgent action network is structured. Their alerts are sent by mail, and not before receiving approval from their London office—a process which can take anywhere from several days to two or more weeks to complete. The realities of El Salvador, however, require almost immediate publicity about an abduction—a sizable response must have been made within the first 72 hours following the abduction, preferably within the first 24 hours—if torture and/or death is to be prevented. Other groups approached with the request declined for reasons usually involving lack of time and resources.

The Presbytery of Chicago, however, kept the idea alive from the time it was approached (November 1983) until April 12, 1984, when by a unanimous voice vote the presbytery undertook to develop the network.

The presbytery originally was approached for at least two major reasons: it has a fairly high national profile, especially among Presbyterians, for its work on Central American issues; and Presbyterians have no churches or other forms of ministry in El Salvador, making them less subject to reprisals because of their involvement in such a project.

The proposal to create the network was discussed by members of the presbytery's Central America Task Force (an action arm of the presbytery's Church and Society Committee), and then by the Church and Society Committee itself. Much of the discussion centered on how the El Salvador office of what came to be known as CUANES would be staffed and operated—issues which cannot be dealt with here because of potential danger to those involved in that office.

Presentation on the floor of the presbytery relied heavily on directives to the presbyteries from the 195th General Assembly (the highest governing body of the Presbyterian Church) meeting in 1983. In a lengthy report on Central America the General Assembly encouraged its presbyteries to explore "mission partnerships" both with ecumenical groups in North America as well as with churches in Central America.[1] CUANES clearly fell under those guidelines.

Contexts

The development of CUANES must be seen as a part of two larger and somewhat overlapping contexts.

In general terms CUANES must be seen in the context of the present reality of El Salvador. And in that reality Christian churches of all denominations are consistently selected as targets for violent persecution by the Salvadoran government and its paramilitary security forces. The cases of Miguel Tomas Castro Garcia and Dr. Angel Ibarra are but two examples of this persecution. In a recent year "there were 14 assassinations of pastors . . ., 41 arbitrary detentions, 14 public defamations of religious authorities and institutions, 3 dynamitings, 4 machine gunnings, 22 forced searches of religious centers, and 3 occupations of church institutions by the military".[2]

The present reality of El Salvador includes a much more generalized atmosphere of violent persecution, however: Amnesty International reports some 40,000 "extrajudicial executions" of civilians, largely at the hands of the Salvadoran military, since 1980.[3] Targets of the persecution were and are to be found among those who speak and act against the injustices of Salvadoran society. The Christian church is numbered among these.

Symptoms of the injustices of Salvadoran society are abundant. The nation is desperately poor, and the poverty is created—i.e. it did not "just happen". Statistics from a recent year include the following: two percent of the population (the "Fourteen Families" or the "oligarchy") controls sixty percent of the land; fifty-eight percent of the population earns $10 per month or less; seventy percent of the children under age five are malnourished; illiteracy among adults runs at fifty percent in the cities and towns, seventy percent in rural areas; sixty-four percent of the urban population lacks sewage facilities; most of the rural population works for just one-third of the year, and rural un- and under-employment hovers around forty-five percent.[4]

These conditions were created with the destruction of indigenous society in El Salvador, including ancient landholding patterns, in the days of the Spanish *conquistadores*. The Indian and, later, "mixed race" population was subjugated and brutalized first by the Spaniards, later by the local elite (albeit of Iberian descent) following Spain's withdrawal in the early 19th century. This elite, or "oligarchy", maintained its privileged position of economic and political power through two instruments of social control: the military, which rules to this day (as the "power behind the throne" in those rare times when civilians hold office[5]); and the Catholic Church.

And social control was needed, for it does not take a Marxist to tell the vast majority of the population they were hungry because their lands had been stolen[6] and now were being used to produce agricultural goods (including food) for export and the short-term profits exports bring rather than for meeting the needs of the people. Abused and hungry people are angry people, and anger in El Salvador—as elsewhere—historically has taken the form both of organizing for political change and of outright rebellion. Both were, and are, met with violent repression by the "oligarchy."

In the mid-twentieth century the Catholic Church, through a series of historic events[7], began to reassess its supposedly "apolitical" role in Salvadoran society. It discovered that its role was in fact highly political, in the sense of blessing the political arrangements favoring the oligarchy, and also was in glaring contradiction to the social teachings of the Catholic Church as well as the biblical witness. Both social teachings and the biblical witness call attention to God's compassion for the poor and summon the Christian church to side with the poor and oppressed in their struggle against all forms of injustice.

When the Catholic Church began to take these teachings seriously, and thus to act accordingly, it found itself increasingly the target of violent persecution formerly reserved for teachers' unions and peasant organizations in El Salvador.

Reference to the biblical witness points up the second of the larger and somewhat overlapping contexts. CUANES was, and is, firmly rooted in a biblical perspective on public life. This perspective in turn has two components: an understanding of what God is doing in the world, and an understanding of the church's role in witnessing to what God is doing.

God's action in the world may be discerned by reference to what this writer calls the "demographics of the Incarnation". The New Testament affirms, and the Christian church always has agreed, God acted in Christ "when the time had fully come" (Galatians 4:4)—meaning God acted at that precise moment in history when all the components of history were exactly positioned for the completion of revelation and the accomplishment of redemption. The "components of history" include those details God found crucial in revealing the divine nature and purpose; and they include the fact that Jesus was a peasant in what today we would call a "Third World" country which existed in political and economic dependency on a world empire. Furthermore it is of the greatest significance that Jesus lived amidst the poorest and most outcast members of his society, naming them (Matthew 5 and Luke 6) as God's favored ones. Jesus came proclaiming God's reign in history (Mark 1:14f), a reign in which life's values and statuses often would be reversed (Mark 10:31); and for this he was put to death on charges of sedition (Luke 23:2-5,38). It appears, furthermore, Jesus saw his life's work as initiating the Jubilee Year in history: for at the beginning of his public ministry he announced (Luke

4:16-21) that radical new beginning of all of society, mandated in the Law of Jubilee (Leviticus 25:8-55), as beginning in him.[8]

Thus the "demographics of the Incarnation" bring to fulfillment the clear witness of the Hebrew Bible as to what God was, and is, about in history. For from the Creation itself, where God is shown as passionately concerned with the human sphere of life; through the Exodus, where God is shown at work on behalf of the suffering poor; through the Law and Prophets, where God's compassion for the poor and oppressed is legislated and proclaimed, the entire biblical story deals with a God who is at work on the side of the world's weakest and most oppressed people. Thus the Incarnation only completes what has been told all along in the Bible.

The second component of this biblical perspective in which CUANES is rooted has to do with an understanding of the church's role in witnessing to what God is about in the world. And this, again, is twofold. The first task involves pointing to, and participating in, what God is doing in history: "The Christian's first task is to discern the transfiguring power of the Lord in the political and social transformations of the age to gather in action around them."[9] And then the church's task involves supporting its various members as these are involved in such a witness in their own situation. Paul (1 Corinthians 12:26) refers to this kind of solidarity when he writes: "If one member suffers, all the members suffer; if one member is honored, all rejoice with it."

The church in El Salvador, reacting to the violence and injustice of its society, has chosen to gather in action around those "political and social formations"; and it has suffered grievously for it. CUANES was born out of the kind of solidarity described by St. Paul—the suffering of North American Christians when one member of the Body of Christ, that in El Salvador, suffers. The network prays and works for that Day when the one member at last is honored, and all the members rejoice.

III. The Network

With the presbytery's final approval the network began to be organized. An office in El Salvador was established and given a full working budget. A second office in North America, that of U.S. Coordinator of CUANES (occupied by this writer), likewise was established.

Not much can be said about the El Salvador office without compromising personal safety. Essentially that office began work to develop relationships with church leadership in the country—from parish ministers and lay leaders to denominational heads—informing them of the existence of the network, and doing whatever seemed necessary to develop a sense of trust in the efficacy of the network. Much of this work had been done prior to the opening of the CUANES office there. Local church leadership already had established an incipient support network; and criteria by which an alert concerning an abducted church worker would be relayed to North America were developed. Those criteria are threefold:

1) the abducted person must be a church worker as defined by the affected denomination—ordained or lay, paid or volunteer, full- or part-time;
2) the abducted person must not be a combatant;
3) ordinarily all internal (Salvadoran) channels for obtaining the abducted person's safe release will have been exhausted before an alert is relayed to North America—although in practice many decisions to involve CUANES have been made on the assumption that internal channels wouldn't work in the first place.

From the beginning it was agreed the entire network would be politically non-aligned: no matter who the abducting body might be—government, rebel or some other party—an alert would be relayed if the three criteria were met. In practice only government security forces have been involved in the abduction of church workers.

Once the decision was made to involve CUANES, a determination of which government offices should be sent telegrams would be made. In practice this has turned out to be the office of the abducting security force, the office of Salvadoran President Jose Napoleon Duarte, and the office of the U.S. Embassy in San Salvador. Initially it was felt the U.S. Embassy should be involved only in rare instances, since their attention to Salvadoran nationals would raise suspicions on the part of the Salvadoran security forces: *i.e.* it would be better for the Embassy to be perceived as acting in response to directives from the U.S. State Department. In practice the Embassy has been involved in all but the first case.

An initial problem faced by the El Salvador office was the technology of relaying an alert. All phone calls made from the country must go through an operator, and that means the risk of being "overheard" is considerable. To date, however, while discussions continue with technical experts on how alerts might be relayed by other means, all alerts have come by telephone.

The initial problems faced by the U.S. office were far safer, but perhaps even more difficult than those faced in El Salvador. In the latter country the need for the network was obvious, and support was quickly (if covertly) forthcoming. In North America, however, the religious public was approached almost "cold" with the concept of the network.

Housekeeping chores formed the content of the first several weeks' work. An Administrative Board composed of a majority of Presbyterians—a requirement of the presbytery—was formed, and a search for a U.S. Coordinator was begun. Ultimately the U.S. Coordinator was chosen from among the board members.

Human rights groups—especially Amnesty International—were consulted as to their experience in conducting urgent action alerts in foreign countries, and a body of preformed wisdom was accumulated against the day the first alert from El Salvador would come. These preliminary discussions formed the basis for what finally became a printed "Participant's Guide" given to every single CUANES participant. The guide detailed the procedures the participants were to follow.

Preliminary publicity and recruiting for the network were a unified process. Existing religious-based Central America groups—*e.g.* the Interreligious Task Force on Central America, based in New York City—were approached with information about the concept behind CUANES, and with requests both for funding support and for the names of persons who might be interested in participating on the network. Part of the rationale behind such approaches involved the hope of building CUANES out of already existing networks, so that the network would become not so much a new network as a simple information clearing house for existing networks. In fact few responses were gleaned from these initial approaches—the "field" of religious-based groups working on Central American issues is heavily glutted, and a new one faces a very difficult task of making its voice and agenda heard—and in practice CUANES initially became a new network.

The event which "made" CUANES proved to be—as the Administrative Board suspected it would—its first alert. In early July 1984 a literacy promoter working for the Archdiocese of San Salvador, Jaime Remberto Canales Fabian, was abducted. Suddenly the CUANES leadership was "selling" not an abstract concept but an actual "live case". The handful of tentatively interested individuals quickly became a small network: almost everyone contacted, even if they withheld any expression of full commitment to the network, at least would respond to a concrete alert and send the requested telegrams. Virtually everyone who worked to help Jaime stayed on the network.

For the first five months the network survived on small contributions. Funding proposals were sent to virtually all major denominations; and once the case of Jaime concluded successfully these proposals quickly were amended to include "An Actual Case". But as is the case with all funding efforts, the decision-making processes are beyond the petitioner's input; and the network waited and prayed through an agonizing period, just barely managing to print minimal numbers of brochures and carry out minimal mailings. One suspects this experience is quite typical of fledgling organizations; and indeed one denominational official quickly reassured the writer that "you just expect to live off individual donations for a long long time in anything like this".

Beyond the skilled contributions of a committed Administrative Board at least two other factors seem to have been important in getting CUANES "off the ground". First and of lesser importance, was the time available to the U.S. Coordinator. While fully employed as a parish minister during the early days of CUANES, this writer nevertheless found himself in parish situations making very few demands on his time; and hence he was able to devote a large amount of time to the initial correspondence needed to get the network moving. Second, and of far greater importance, was the network's second alert: Miguel Tomas Castro Garcia. Several months had elapsed after Jaime's release, and the U.S. Coordinator nurtured a private uneasiness about the real extent of the need for the network—not to mention the problem of maintaining morale and interest levels high during prolonged periods when "nothing was happening". But then came the dreadful afternoon of October 28, 1984; and the abduction of Miguel Tomas proved to be not "just another abduction". The Salvadoran Baptist pastor was well known in church circles throughout North America, and a number of U.S. congregations as well as some in Canada had formed "sister church" relationships with Emmanuel Baptist. So when word of the alert was relayed to North America CUANES faced a new and entirely unexpected problem: at times the volume of phone calls coming to the U.S. Coordinator's office, even in the wee hours of the morning, conveying questions about how to help Miguel became so heavy it often was hard to keep the existing network activated. Entire church-based networks joined in the effort; one, on its own initiative, occupied a Salvadoran Consulate—an event which "turned" the case, for that prompted a panicky consular staff to call President Duarte who in turn called the U.S. Embassy.

The case of Miguel Tomas clearly proved CUANES' efficacy, for there is no doubt that the combined efforts of persons and groups acting through—and on behalf of—the network quickly secured Miguel's release. CUANES also became internationalized, for the Baptist pastor was well-known in several other countries (including England, Canada and Australia); and existing networks joined with CUANES to work for Miguel's release, then stayed to participate in the network on all future alerts.

The El Salvador office of CUANES has proved to be, with the exception of Miguel's case, the best recruiting source for the network. Virtually every visiting church person encounters the CUANES people there, whether they know it or not; and those who seem likely "candidates" for the network quietly are introduced to it, and are steered to the U.S. Coordinator for further information. Outside the support garnered during individual alerts it seems likely seventy percent of the network traces its "origin" to contact with the El Salvador office. Probably that statistic would change somewhat if the U.S. Coordinator's position were a full-time position, and the Coordinator had the time to do all necessary publicity for the network on top of other commitments; but such is not the case, and for better or worse publicity has depended on the El Salvador office, individual alerts, and attendant "word of mouth" promotion.

The composition of the network follows no clear pattern. Presbyterians, despite the presbytery's involvement, do not compose a major segment of the network. Heavy involvement comes from Lutherans, Quakers and the United Church of Christ—where denominational affiliation can be determined. Reasons for this particular kind of representation are unclear. Lutherans are involved in El Salvador in many ways; the United Church of Christ is not involved at all.

Currently the network numbers perhaps 700 members in the U.S., with as yet indeterminate numbers on the English, Canadian, Taiwanese and Australian networks of already-existing church solidarity groups. (These total perhaps 250-500 persons.) Some assessment of the volume of response for a given alert is made by using a common telegram company based in California; but many members continue to use Western Union, others can't afford telegrams and so make phone calls and/or send letters, and in general it remains difficult to determine the total response in any individual case.

Currently efforts are underway to find State Coordinators to whom would be referred all inquiries about the network from persons in their state, and to whose oversight the phone tree network in their state would be remanded. At present perhaps one-third of those asked to be State Coordinators have agreed, one-third have declined because of the obvious amount of work involved, and one-third have made no commitment.

All network participants are encouraged to develop their own phone tree(s) and then inform the U.S. Coordinator of the names and mailing addresses of those persons involved (the fact that total network membership is as yet indeterminate reflects the difficulty in eliciting this kind of response). All participants then receive full field reports on each case from the El Salvador office—reports sent to the U.S. office by courier within two to four weeks of the closing of the case. In the future it is hoped a "newsletter" will become available, containing the (anonymous) reflections of the El Salvador office as well as (anonymous) writings—theological and literary—from Salvadoran church persons.

IV. Evaluation

In its first 11 months of operations CUANES has demonstrated several clear strengths as well as several unresolved question areas (*i.e.* areas where questions remain unanswered). An evaluation will proceed by naming the one most obvious strength of the network, followed by an enumeration of the question areas, followed by an enumeration of the remaining strengths.

The most promising strength of the network is indicated in the title of this paper: it represents a model for an entirely new form of public ministry for the church. When one considers the successes encountered to date by CUANES in its limited history and field of action (*i.e.* restricted to Salvadoran church workers); and when simultaneously one considers the various forms of repression suffered by the church in other parts of the world (*e.g.* Poland, South Africa, the Soviet Union etc.) an entirely new form of ministry opens up. Other human rights groups (*e.g.* Amnesty International) focus on religious workers, and allow participants to "specialize" in that area; but so far as is known to this writer, none has the capacity to respond almost instantaneously by virtue of telephone alerts—a vital necessity in El Salvador, and indeed throughout the world. And in fact representatives of several U.S. denomonations already are being consulted about the possibility of expanding the network throughout Central America, with country-specific backing by a denomination not otherwise involved in that country. The details of how CUANCA (the Christian Urgent Action Network for Central America), later to be replaced by CUANLA (the Christian Urgent Action Network for Latin America), might operate are beyond the scope of this paper; but the clear and evident model lies at hand in CUANES.

Nevertheless some unresolved questions remain; and these must at least be articulated, if not fully answered, if CUANES is to improve its effectiveness and if the network is to be expanded usefully in some way. They include the following:

1) The "effect" of CUANES is unknown in any precise way. Are the "successes" to date in fact due to the network's intervention, or are they simple coincidence? It may be impossible ever to answer this question, as even Amnesty International will acknowledge when confronted with the same issue. The inner workings of governments and their security forces remain closed to discernment and analysis.

2) There always is the question of why the network deals only with church workers, when tens of thousands of ordinary people also are numbered among the "disappeared". These latter lack even the nominal backing of an institution such as the Christian church in some form. Thus CUANES to some appears "elitist"—a suggestion quite bothersome to both the U.S. and El Salvador offices of the network. The moral issue of evident "elitism" is buttressed by the problems which are created when many segments of the church, not to mention the general secular and/or non-Christian religious public, are alienated by such appearances and thus cannot be recruited for the network.

3) The supposed "safety factor" of having a denomination such as the Presbyterian Church, not otherwise present in El Salvador, involved in the network in fact may be illusory. There remains the constant possibility of indirect represal. Salvadoran security forces may at any time focus repression against one segment of the Salvadoran religious community and make certain the Presbyterians know this will last until they "back off"—surely as effective as targeting Presbyterians for overt violence. And likewise it remains a real possibility—with ample historical precedent[10]—that security forces in El Salvador might work out an agreement with their counterparts in, say, Guatemala whereby Presbyterians in the latter country would be singled out for repression until the denomination "backed off" in El Salvador.

4) There remains the unresolved question of possible over-response. Miguel Tomas later reported, from his exile in Mexico, that at one point his interrogators implied he "must" be a guerrilla of some considerable importance—or else he wouldn't be getting all this "international attention". While nothing evident came of that, the CUANES network found itself worrying a great deal over whether too much publicity can become counterproductive. In subsequent weeks following Miguel's "arrest" and release three incidents occurred which raised fears even higher. In two of them lay church workers were abducted, held overnight and interrogated during beatings, and then released the next morning (one of them was from Emmanuel Baptist Church). In a third incident a Lutheran pastor was abducted, tortured and murdered in the space of a few hours (CUANES was asked to intervene in the form of publicizing the murder and demanding

an investigation: it did, and two army officers subsequently were arrested and charged). All three incidents raised the fears that the "success" of the network with Miguel Tomas had forced the security forces to change their *modus operendi* to "quick hits": abduction, beating, interrogation followed by release or assassination—all carried out too quickly for CUANES to intervene. While five months have elapsed since these three incidents occurred, during which time four more "regular" abductions have taken place (and all resolved successfully) with no further "quick hits", concern remains.

5) An agonizing unresolved question remains: at what personal danger does the El Salvador office work? What would be the effect on the efficacy of the network of an abduction involving the office there? While some ingenious safety precautions are built into the work of the El Salvador office, this grim possibility remains to haunt and disturb those who realize what is at stake. Those who work in the El Salvador office literally are asked to put their lives on the line. It is a terribly difficult request to make, a terribly difficult decision to live with.

Given these serious and perhaps unanswerable questions, the network remains with some obvious strengths—ones which, in the opinion of this writer, greatly outweigh the questions. These strengths include the following:

1) Despite the first unanswered question articulated above, it appears rather obvious the network "works". The claim is made on two grounds.

First, in the case of Miguel Tomas Castro Garcia we became privy to things said within the security force system. His interrogators asked him why he was getting so much international attention, as indicated previously; and in the discussion with Baptist leaders held by the Director of National Police (p. 94) the Director asked the church leaders not to create any further "international incidents"—a discussion relayed verbatim to the CUANES El Salvador office and included in its final report.

Second, as Amnesty International and other such groups have observed, when pressure in the form of publicity is exerted the abducted have a tendency to reappear, but when such pressure is lacking the abducted tend not to reappear.

Miguel himself today is quite explicit in saying the network saved his life; and perhaps there can be no greater confirmation than that.

2) The network provides "ordinary Christians" with an immediate and tangible—and life-saving!—way of participating in the larger ministry of the church. "Mission fields" can be remote, accessible only to the imaginative ruminations of the mind; but the "mission field" of a project such as CUANES is as accessible as a phone call to the telegram company.

A kind of corollary to this observation is found in reply to the frustration North Americans feel when they encounter the suffering and injustice in another part of the world, but then face the inevitable and enervating question: "But what can I do?" Central America, in this case, is far away; the legislative processes through which change might come are so complicated and perhaps cumbersome. But CUANES provides something an individual can *do*: and to that extent it is imbued with personal meaning and urgency.

3) The network strengthens the participants' sense of the unity of the Body of Christ. One becomes intensely, emotionally involved in the plight of churches in El Salvador as, through individual abduction cases, one comes to realize the extent of the church's suffering. The words of Paul (1 Corinthians 12:26, quoted on p. 97) find uncanny fulfillment.

Such feelings work in reverse. When a CUANES Board member "happened" to enter Emmanuel Baptist Church during Miguel's abduction—he had come to El Salvador on personal business and had no idea the crisis was underway—he was identified by others present in terms of his CUANES connections. He was greeted with a thunderous ovation. The experience is one this gentle and rather self-effacing individual never will forget.

4) The network raises consciousness and educates church persons about the realities of Central America. Sooner or later network participants realize only government security forces torture and kill Christians; and even the most politically uninvolved begin to ask questions. As alerts are pursued through recommended channels, participants get a hands-on civics lesson in how diplomatic channels work, how power works at national and international levels, and, for some, the disturbing experience of the difference between public statements and official versions versus reality. It is revealing to receive a letter from the U.S. Embassy concerning an abduction in which what amounts to the Salvadoran government's version of events is given uncritically and then to compare this with the CUANES report composed of eyewitness testimony, including that of the abducted person. The latter version, of course, might be subject to manipulation by those with propaganda lines to sell; but the character of the denominational leadership involved in the decision to issue a CUANES alert, combined with the exhaustive care taken by the El Salvador office in composing the field report, makes such a thing highly unlikely in this writer's opinion.

A case in point involves the recent torture/murder of a Lutheran pastor (see p. 101). The U.S. Embassy immediately charged "the guerrillas" with the crime; the El Salvador office of CUANES tentatively reacted accordingly; and the U.S. network began the process of confronting the rebel offices in North America. Those directly involved in El Salvador continued to probe and to ask hard questions. Suddenly the Salvadoran government arrested two army officers and charged them with the crime, and the Embassy quietly and without apology or explanation changed its story accordingly. A similar incident involves the case of Miguel Tomas Castro Garcia: to this day the Embassy maintains Miguel confessed his involvement with the guerrillas, while (see p. 94) the National Police Director admitted there were no grounds to substantiate a case against him.

5) The network strengthens the church in its role in a repressive society. The Christian community in El Salvador is the conscience of the nation in a way perhaps difficult to imagine in secular North America; and its voice strengthens the work of all persons and groups working for a more just society. The backing of CUANES greatly strengthens the willingness of individual Christians to take the risks involved in taking the side of the oppressed. In fact such publicity as CUANES may generate may be the only non-violent means left for staying the hand of the oppressor. Thus the church is made bold to "discern the transfiguring power of the Lord in the political and social formations of the age and to gather in power around them."

But finally ministry deals with individual persons and their stories. Therefore it is fitting to close with perhaps the best evaluation of CUANES there could be: a personal, hand-written note from Miguel Tomas Castro Garcia. Sent to this writer by courier and intended for the network which he says saved his life, the note read:

> Receive my expression of sincere gratitude. I can say that the Lord has heard our prayers and that the Christians of the world have given a testimonial of fraternity

before their Savior and the world community. For all this may our God be praised! On behalf of my wife, my children, my mother and myself, receive our very heart as a token of our gratitude. Your brother and debtor from the bottom of this heart which the Lord has blessed,

(Signed) Miguel Tomas.

1. 195th General Assembly of the Presbyterian Church (U.S.A.), *Adventure and Hope: Christians and the Crisis in Central America* (New York: General Assembly of the Presbyterian Church [U.S.A.], 1983), pp. 45-46.
2. *Ibid.*, p.35.
3. Amnesty International, *Extrajudicial Executions in El Salvador: Report of an Amnesty International Mission to Examine Post-Mortem and Investigative Procedures in Political Killings, 1-6 July 1983* (New York: Amnesty International Publications, 1984), p. 3.
4. Robert Armstrong and Janet Shenk, *El Salvador: The Face of Revolution* (Boston: South End Press, 1982), pp. 6-7.
5. This is a basic and heavily-documented argument made by Raymond Bonner in *Weakness and Deceit: U.S. Policy and El Salvador* (New York: Times Books, the New York Times Book Co., Inc., 1984).
6. The process by which land was stolen from peasants is told succinctly in Armstrong and Shenk, *El Salvador,* pp. 5-6.
7. For perhaps the best overall review of this process see Penny Lernoux, *Cry of the People: The Struggle for Human Rights in Latin America—The Catholic Church in Conflict With U.S. Policy* (New York: Penguin Books, 1982).
8. John Howard Yoder, *The Politics of Jesus* (Grand Rapids, MI: William B. Eerdmans Publishing Co., 1972), pp. 64-77. See also Thomas D. Hanks, *God So Loved the Third World: The Biblical Vocabulary of Oppression* (Maryknoll, NY: Orbis Books, 1983), pp. 97-108.
9. William R. Coats, *God in Public: Political Theology Beyond Niebuhr* (Grand Rapids, MI: William B. Eerdmans Publishing Co., 1974), p. 56.
10. Armstrong and Shenk, *El Salvador,* pp. 216-218.

Notes about the Contributors

Ann Bartram teaches pastoral counseling at the Toronto School of Theology and is Director of Training at the Toronto Institute of Human Relations. She is a graduate of the University of Western Ontario. She received her B.D. from Victoria University and her D.Min. from the Chicago Theological Seminary.

Steven F. Durham is currently Director and Resource Developer for "Centro Romero," a self-help organization for Central American refugees in the Chicago metropolitan area. He also serves as the U.S. Coordinator for the project described in his paper in this volume. He holds a B.A. from the University of Missouri, a M.Div. from McCormick Theological Seminary, and a D.Min. from the Chicago Theological Seminary.

Gary S. Gerson is Rabbi of the Oak Park Temple B'nai Abraham Zion. He received a B.A. from the University of Michigan, an M.A. in religion and an M.A. in psychology from Temple University, and a D.Min. from the Chicago Theological Seminary.

Renny Golden is Assistant Professor of Criminal Justice at Northeastern Illinois University. She received a B.A. from Siena Heights College, a M.Ed. from Wayne State University, and a D.Min from the Chicago Theological Seminary.

Robert B. Hurst is a minister of St. Paul's United Church of Christ, Monee, Illinois. He holds a B.A. from Trinity College, a M.Div. from Yale University, and a D.Min.from the Chicago Theological Seminary.

Roy H. May, Jr. has been a Methodist missionary engaged in rural development and theological education programs in Bolivia. He has been a visiting professor at the seminary in San José Costa Rica and is currently a visiting professor at St. Paul School of Theology in Kansas City. He received a B.A. and M.Th. from Southern Methodist University and a D.Min. from the Chicago Theological Seminary.

Felix Sugirtharaj is engaged in educational and church work in India. He holds a B.A. from the University of Madras, a Diploma in Theology from United Theological College (India), a M.S.T. from Union Theological Seminary (New York) and a D.Min. from the Chicago Theological Seminary.